A LITERARY FEAST

Recipes inspired by novels, poems and plays

JENNIFER BARCLAY

summersdale

A LITERARY FEAST

Summersdale Publishers Ltd
46 West Street
Chichester
West Sussex
PO19 1RP
UK

www.summersdale.com

Printed and bound in the Czech Republic

ISBN: 978-1-84953-737-7

Substantial discounts on bulk quantities of Summersdale books are available to corporations, professional associations and other organisations. For details contact Nicky Douglas by telephone: +44 (0) 1243 756902, fax: +44 (0) 1243 786300 or email: nicky@summersdale.com.

CONTENTS

Disclaimer

The recipes in this book are compiled as a culinary complement
to popular literature, and the author and publisher cannot
guarantee the accuracy or success of every recipe.

INTRODUCTION

*'For eating and reading are two pleasures
that combine admirably.'*

C. S. Lewis

Irish poet Jonathan Swift's poem 'How Shall I Dine' shows an utterly charming scene of a man carefully preparing his good quality mutton for the fire, spreading the cloth on the table and sharpening the knives. One way we judge and understand characters in literature is by the food they eat and how they eat it. In a play written by Euripides in the fifth century BC, we comprehend the grief felt by Medea after her husband Jason takes another woman when we hear: 'She lies without food and gives herself up to suffering'. The hedonistic excesses of the Egyptian court of Cleopatra that have lured the noble Roman Antony away from his duties are conjured by Shakespeare in the incredulous exchange:

MECENAS: Eight wild boars roasted whole at a breakfast, and but twelve persons there. Is this true?

DOMITIUS ENOBARBUS: This was but as a fly by an eagle: we had much more monstrous matter of feast.

How people think about food also makes a character unique. Who but Marian McAlpin, in Margaret Atwood's first novel *The Edible Woman*, would think, as she chews a forkful of sponge cake, that 'it felt spongy and cellular against her tongue, like the bursting of thousands of tiny lungs'?

We know people not only by what and how they eat but also by how they cook. In her 2003 novel *Crescent*, Diana Abu Jaber writes that tasting a piece of bread that someone has baked 'is like looking out of their eyes'. Cooking is a pleasure that connects us across centuries and cultures, so that when we read the Chinese poet Bai Juyi (or Po Chu-i), who lived 772–846, describe 'Eating Bamboo Shoots', we can identify with his glee at finding himself in a place where they are abundant and cheap, and we are almost there inhaling the steam when he boils them in an earthen pot until the white skin opens 'like new pearls'.

In this book, I have had the pleasure of uncovering some memorable scenes of food in well-loved literature from around the world – plays, poetry and novels – and pairing them with recipes so you can make your own literary feasts. I hope that grazing through this menu of culinary bon mots will give you as much enjoyment and satisfaction as I gleaned from preparing it.

'You must sit down,' says Love, 'and taste my meat.'

So I did sit and eat.

From 'Love', George Herbert

STARTERS
AND SNACKS

To skip to Mains, go to p.71

TROCHILUS: *At times he wants to eat a dish of loach from Phalerum; I seize my dish and fly to fetch him some. Again he wants some pea soup; I seize a ladle and a pot and run to get it.*

The Birds, Aristophanes

EASY-PEASY SOUP FOR A DISCERNING PALATE

In this comic play from classical Greece, Trochilus, the 'errand-bird' is slave to Epops, a man who was turned into a hoopoe bird and asked his servant also to turn into a bird so he could continue to serve him. There's nothing bird-like about his appetite, clearly.

Serves 8

Ingredients

....

1 tbsp butter
1 tbsp extra virgin olive oil
1 medium onion or 2
  spring onions
1 stalk celery
2 cloves chopped garlic
1 tsp chopped fresh mint

1.2 kg peas, fresh or frozen
1 litre stock (vegetable or
  chicken)
Salt and pepper

Optional:
Pine nuts

Preparation

....

1. Heat the oil and butter over a medium heat until the butter has melted.

2. Chop the onion and celery, and cook for several minutes until softened. Stir garlic and mint into the mix, and cook for a minute.

3. Add the peas and stock, increase the heat and bring to a simmer, then lower the heat and keep at a simmer for a minute or two until the peas are tender.

4. Blend until smooth, adding salt and pepper to taste.

5. Toast the pine nuts in a dry frying pan, if using, and sprinkle on top as a garnish.

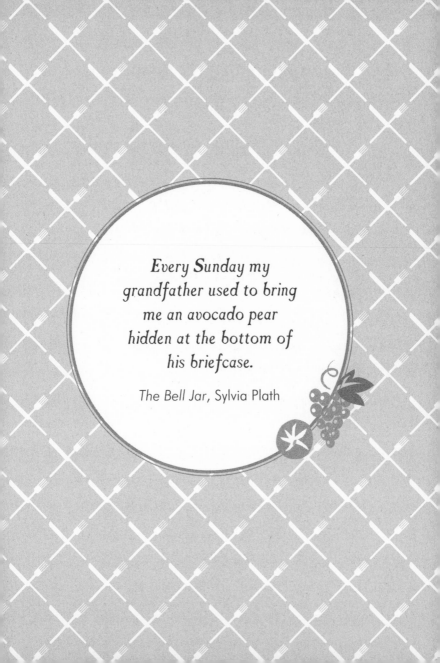

Every Sunday my grandfather used to bring me an avocado pear hidden at the bottom of his briefcase.

The Bell Jar, Sylvia Plath

AVOCADO WITH GRAPE JELLY DRESSING

A luncheon of avocado and crabmeat salad makes Esther remember her grandfather, who was head waiter at a country club and used to sneak home treats for her. The avocado arrived under the 'six soiled shirts and the Sunday comics' in his briefcase, and he served it with grape jelly vinaigrette.

Serves 2

Ingredients

1 avocado, halved, stone removed
Handful of cooked and shelled prawns, chopped
Small ruby grapefruit, chopped
2 tsp grape or any red fruit jelly, e.g. redcurrant jelly
2 tsp lemon juice
1 tbsp olive oil

Preparation

1. Mix the jelly, juice and oil into a dressing.

2. Fill both cups of the avocado pear with a mixture of prawns and grapefruit, and drench in dressing.

3. Serve with spoons.

POINS: Item, a capon, two shillings and twopence.
Item, sauce, fourpence.
Item, sack, two gallons, five shillings and eightpence.
Item, anchovies, and sack after supper, two shillings and sixpence.
Item, bread a halfpenny.
PRINCE HENRY: O monstrous! But one halfpenny worth of bread to this intolerable deal of sack!

Henry IV, Part I, William Shakespeare

ANCHOVIES AND ROASTED RED PEPPERS FOR A FALSTAFFIAN APPETITE

Falstaff is asleep behind the arras, 'snorting like a horse', when Prince Henry and his men search his pockets and find receipts from his last few meals out. Falstaff washed his anchovies down with 'sack', a semi-fortified wine imported from Spain or its islands, not unlike what we today call sherry; here we add a little sherry vinegar for flavour – it won't leave your guests snorting like horses.

Serves 4

Ingredients

4 large red peppers (pimientos) or equivalent quantity
   from jar
Head of garlic
2 tbsp olive oil
1 tbsp sherry vinegar
Salt and pepper
8 slices of crusty bread
8 small anchovy fillets (use the best quality you can find)

Preparation

....

1. If you're preparing the peppers yourself, roast them whole under the grill in the oven for approximately 20 minutes or over a naked flame, turning until the skins are evenly charred all over. If you roast the peppers in the oven, put the head of garlic in to roast too with the top sliced off. Otherwise, roast the garlic by itself at 180°C for 20 minutes, until the cloves are soft.

2. Remove the peppers from the heat and allow them to cool in a bowl covered with a lid, or a plastic bag, for 15 minutes so that the steam helps the skin to separate from the flesh.

3. Remove the skins from the flesh, and scoop out the seedy insides using your hand or a knife, and discard, retaining as much juice as possible.

4. Cut the remaining fleshy parts of the peppers into thirds or smaller, toss in oil and sherry vinegar, season with salt and pepper and set aside.

5. Spread a little roasted garlic on each slice of bread. (If you're using peppers from a jar or roasting them on a naked flame, you can chop a few cloves of garlic and add to the red peppers in oil and vinegar.)

6. Arrange the pieces of pepper on the bread, topping off with a couple of anchovy fillets and a little juice from the pepper mix.

Shakespeare's Glutton

Though there are plenty of general references to 'cakes and ale' and foodstuffs like garlic and onions, there is little eating seen in Shakespeare's plays, except where the portly Falstaff appears in *Henry IV* and in *The Merry Wives of Windsor*. Falstaff is Shakespeare's legendary glutton, with a vast appetite for food and drink which is one of the things that makes him, in spite of being vain and cowardly, a loveable rogue. He spends much time drinking at the Boar's Head tavern.

He was one of Shakespeare's most popular characters in his day, and remains so today, often being brought into productions of *Henry V* even though he has no lines in the actual play. Later works inspired by Shakespeare's character (which may itself have been based on earlier versions) include Antonio Salieri's 1799 opera *Falstaff*, Giuseppe Verdi's 1893 opera of the same name, and James White's *Falstaff's Letters* of 1796.

When I lift a forkful of vegetables they glisten like faceted jewels, uniformly cut.

Hunger, Jane Ward

GRILLED SALMON WITH SALSA TOO GOOD TO LEAVE ON THE PLATE

Anna, a gifted cook, prepares this dish to perfection specially for her husband, hoping to get his attention, but he falls asleep over the plate, and she eats it herself. I would too. Being very particular, she removes any stray bones from the salmon beforehand with needle-nose pliers.

Serves 4

Ingredients

4 small fillets of salmon
1 small cucumber, peeled
2 plum tomatoes
1 small red pepper
1 medium red onion
1 avocado
Juice of 1 lime
Handful fresh coriander or cilantro
1 dollop wholegrain mustard

Preparation

1. First make the salsa, dicing all the vegetables uniformly and tossing with lime juice and coriander or cilantro so that they glisten like jewels.

2. Remove any stray bones from the salmon, then brush with the mustard before grilling it. Whether grilling on a barbecue or in an oven, use a slightly oiled rack or pan to prevent sticking, and grill the skin side first, then flip, for about 4 or 5 minutes each side depending on the heat and thickness of the pieces. The salmon should be browned on the outside and retain a little pink inside.

3. Serve with the salsa.

Fair fa' your honest, sonsie face,
Great chieftain o' the puddin'-race!
Aboon them a' ye tak your place,
Painch, tripe, or thairm:
Weel are ye worthy o' a grace
As lang's my arm.

From 'Address to a Haggis', Robert Burns

HAGGIS-STUFFED MUSHROOMS

*Reader, your time would be better spent reading Robert
Burns or writing poetry than actually making your own
haggis. It's far too much effort. But here's an interesting
way to serve it, for a change from tatties and neeps.
If you use vegetarian haggis, this makes a great non-
meat starter; for vegans, omit the cheese. If you use
smaller mushrooms, they make fine bite-sized snacks.*

Serves 8 (or 3–4 as a main course, served
with salad and a dram of whisky)

Ingredients

Few generous glugs of olive oil
2 cloves garlic, finely chopped
400 g haggis, removed from casing
40 g pine nuts
1 tbsp fresh chopped marjoram or parsley
Salt and ground black pepper
8 large flat portobello mushrooms
40 g breadcrumbs or crumbled oatcakes
40 g Parmesan, pecorino or sharp Cheddar

Preparation

....

1. Heat the oven to 200°C.

2. Wash the mushrooms and dry carefully, remove the stalks but don't discard.

3. Warm the olive oil in a frying pan and gently sauté the garlic for 5 minutes.

4. Chop the mushroom stalks and add them to the pan.

5. Add the haggis, pine nuts and marjoram or parsley, and stir to heat through, adding in salt and pepper to taste.

6. Fill the mushrooms with the haggis mixture.

7. Sprinkle with breadcrumbs and cheese, and bake on a baking sheet or in a gratin dish in the oven for 20 minutes or until golden brown.

To make this condiment, your poet begs
The pounded yellow of two hard-boiled eggs;
Two boiled potatoes, passed through kitchen sieve,
Smoothness and softness to the salad give.
Let onion atoms lurk within the bowl,
And, half suspected, animate the whole.
Of mordant mustard add a single spoon,
Distrust the condiment that bites so soon;
But deem it not, thou man of herbs, a fault,
To add a double quantity of salt;
Four times the spoon with oil from Lucca crown,
And twice with vinegar, procured from town;
And, lastly, o'er the flavoured compound toss
A magic soupçon of anchovy sauce.
O green and glorious! O herbaceous treat!
'T would tempt the dying anchorite to eat.

From 'A Recipe for Salad', Sydney Smith

EGG AND POTATO
HERBACEOUS TREAT SALAD

*Sydney Smith's doggerel poem made the recipe
for this starter easy to memorise. Retaining the
essence of the recipe, I have left out the pounding
and sieving, and added a little rocket. The Lucca
region of Italy produces a superior olive oil.*

Serves 2

Ingredients

....

4–6 new potatoes
2 spring onions
2 handfuls of rocket leaves
  or green beans
Salt and pepper

3 eggs
1 tbsp extra virgin olive oil
1 tsp wholegrain mustard
1 tsp anchovy sauce

Preparation

....

1. Boil and then halve the potatoes.

2. Chop the onions finely.

3. Roughly tear the rocket leaves or steam the green beans.

4. Toss the onions with the potatoes and rocket or green beans lightly, seasoning with salt and pepper.

5. Hard-boil the eggs, cut them in halves and arrange neatly on top, and drizzle with a dressing made from the oil, mustard and anchovy sauce.

Souls of Poets dead and gone,
What Elysium have ye known,
Happy field or mossy cavern,
Choicer than the Mermaid Tavern?
Have ye tippled drink more fine
Than mine host's Canary wine?
Or are fruits of Paradise
Sweeter than those dainty pies
Of venison? O generous food!
Drest as though bold Robin Hood
Would, with his maid Marian,
Sup and bowse from horn and can.

From 'Lines on a Mermaid Tavern', John Keats

DAINTY, BOOZY VENISON PIES FIT FOR THE MERMAID TAVERN

The red wine gives these dainty venison pies a flavour of the tavern which inspired the great poet. The Mermaid stood on Cheapside in London in Elizabethan times, and Ben Jonson and John Donne were among those who frequented a drinking club at the establishment, which would sadly burn down during the Great Fire of London.

Serves 8

Ingredients

3 tbsp olive oil
750 g venison, diced finely
2 tbsp flour
100 g bacon pieces or pancetta cubes
2 small onions, chopped
2 garlic cloves, chopped
Large glass red wine
250 g pumpkin, peeled and diced
2 medium carrots, diced
400 g can chopped tomatoes
300 ml beer
1 kg ready rolled shortcrust pastry
Sprig rosemary
Sprig thyme
Bay leaf

Preparation

....

1. Heat half the oil in an ovenproof casserole dish, add onion, garlic, carrot and pumpkin, and cook on a low to medium heat until softening.

2. Add the bacon/pancetta for a few minutes, then the herbs and a little of the flour and stir together.

3. Add tomatoes and beer, and stir again well, ensuring nothing sticks to the bottom of the dish. Set aside.

4. Dredge the venison lightly in the remaining flour and brown it in the oil in a large frying pan over a medium heat.

5. Transfer the venison to the casserole dish, then deglaze the frying pan with the red wine (take a swig first, toasting Keats), allowing it to bubble, and pour over the meat and vegetables, mixing all the ingredients well, adding a little water if more liquid is needed.

6. Place in the oven at 160°C or simmer on the stove for around 2½ hours until the meat is tender and the sauce thickened.

7. Leave overnight in the fridge.

8. Grease mini pie dishes (muffin/cupcake tins will do) generously with butter, greasing the top of the pan also, and preheat oven to 180°C.

9. Roll the pastry on a floured surface to a thickness of approximately 3 mm and cut to fit the pie dishes, enough

to leave a slight overhang when the pastry is firmly pressed to the sides. Cut the lids to fit. Brush the overhang with beaten egg yolk.

10. Spoon the meat filling into the cases, place the pastry lids on and crimp the edges to seal, and brush the tops with egg yolk to glaze.

11. Bake for 25–30 minutes until golden.

12. Allow to cool, and then use a knife to ease the pies out of the tins.

A sweet, acidulous, down-reaching thrill
Pervades my sense. I seem to see or hear
The lushy garden-grounds of Greenwich Hill
In autumn, where the crispy leaves are sere;
And odours haunt me of remotest spice
From the Levant or musky-aired Cathay,
Or from the saffron-fields of Jericho,
Where everything is nice.
The more I sniff, the more I swoon away,
And what else mortal palate craves, forego.

Odours unsmelled are keen, but those I smell
Are keener; wherefore let me sniff again!
Enticing walnuts, I have known ye well
In youth, when pickles were a passing pain;
Unwitting youth, that craves the candy stem,
And sugar-plums to olives doth prefer,
And even licks the pots of marmalade
When sweetness clings to them:
But now I dream of ambergris and myrrh,
Tasting these walnuts in the poplar shade.

From 'Ode on a Jar of Pickles', Bayard Taylor

SALAD WITH PICKLED WALNUTS AND CHEESE

Bayard Taylor was paying homage to the literary giant Keats when he wrote this hilariously over the top poem about a jar of pickles. But why not wax lyrical about pickles?

Serves 2

Ingredients

4 tomatoes
2 small apples
2 stalks celery, with leaves
Handful salad leaves
Generous slice of crumbly cheese, e.g. bleu d'Auvergne, Cheshire or feta

2 or 3 pickled walnuts, chopped
2 tbsp extra virgin olive oil
2 tsp cider or white wine vinegar
1 tsp Dijon mustard

Preparation

1. Slice the tomatoes, apple and celery, chop the celery leaves and add them all to the salad leaves.

2. Scatter the walnuts on top and crumble the cheese over.

3. Drizzle generously with dressing made from the olive oil, vinegar and mustard.

But Stepan Arkadyevitch, though he was used to different kinds of dinners, found everything excellent, the herb-beer, the bread, the butter, and especially the cold chicken, the mushrooms, the cabbage-soup, the fowl with white sauce, and the white Krimean wine, everything was admirable, wonderful!

Anna Karenina, Leo Tolstoy

MUSHROOM PÂTÉ

Stepan ate and admired a kind of salted or marinated mushrooms: mushrooms were traditionally gathered wild, as in Anna Karenina, and then boiled and kept in some combination of oil, vinegar, garlic, salt and spices. This simple vegetarian pâté based on a Russian dish can be made with fresh mushrooms and is also an excellent hors d'oeuvre or picnic food. Quantities can be adjusted according to taste.

Serves 6–8

Ingredients

....

1 kg mushrooms
2 onions
2 tbsp olive oil, or 1 tbsp oil and 1 tbsp butter
1½ tsp salt
Black pepper
Optional:
Small handful walnuts
120 ml sour cream or cream cheese

Preparation

....

1. Heat the oil in a large frying pan. Add the onions, finely sliced, and sauté until softening and turning translucent.

2. Add the mushrooms and stir-fry until they are turning soft and deep brown.

3. Mix in the salt to taste, and then remove from heat.

4. If you are adding walnuts, chop these finely and put in a food processor, then add in the other ingredients, including the sour cream or cream cheese if desired, and mince to a pâté – it doesn't need to be too smooth.

5. Serve warm or cold with black pepper.

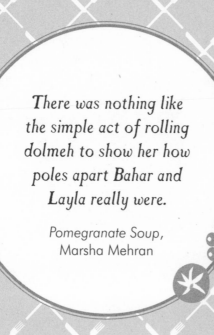

There was nothing like the simple act of rolling dolmeh to show her how poles apart Bahar and Layla really were.

Pomegranate Soup,
Marsha Mehran

PERSIAN DOLMEH

There are many variations on stuffed vine leaves, cabbage leaves or other vegetables from Greece to the Middle East; the Persian variety is called dolmeh (similar to the Greek dolmades). Fresh herbs are important – in Pomegranate Soup, *they are made with fresh tarragon, mint and summer savory. Marjan uses her 'entire torso' to mix the flavours thoroughly. The dolmeh go very well with a cucumber and yoghurt dip, such as tzatziki. Serve with Irish stout to get the Irish–Iranian cultural mix from the book.*

To make 20 dolmeh (serves 4–6)

Ingredients

....

Olive oil
1 onion, chopped
1 clove garlic, minced
125 g minced lamb or beef
1 tbsp each of fresh summer savory, dill, tarragon and mint
  (parsley or basil can be used as substitutes)
Juice of 2 limes
570 g cooked long-grain rice
Salt and pepper
20 canned vine leaves in brine, rinsed, with any vine stems
  removed from the leaves

Preparation

....

1. Warm the olive oil in a frying pan and brown the meat with the chopped onion and garlic.

2. Chop the herbs, add to pan and fry for 3 minutes, then empty the mixture into a bowl with the rice, lime juice, and a good pinch of salt and a few grinds of pepper, and mix well.

3. Place a spoonful of the mixture in the middle of a vine leaf and roll from the base, folding in the sides, so that the filling is sealed inside the leaf.

4. Repeat to use all the filling.

5. Grease a baking dish and, with the dolmeh seam side down, fill the dish so that they make a snug fit, adding 80 ml water, then cover tightly in foil.

6. Bake in the oven for 45 minutes at 110°C.

But when that smoking chowder came in, the mystery was delightfully explained. Oh! Sweet friends, hearken to me. It was made of small juicy clams, scarcely bigger than hazelnuts, mixed with pounded ship biscuits and salted pork cut up into little flakes! the whole enriched with butter, and plentifully seasoned with pepper and salt.

Moby-Dick, Herman Melville

NEW ENGLAND CLAM CHOWDER

*The landlord of the Spouter-Inn recommended Cousin
Hosea at the Try Pots, famous for his chowders, but Ishmael,
having never tasted one before, was puzzled by Hosea's wife's
question 'Clam or cod?', thinking a single clam shared between
him and his companion being a 'rather cold and clammy
reception' and a 'cheerless prospect'. If you've never tasted
clam chowder either, you don't know what you're missing.*

Serves 4

Ingredients

....

2 slices bacon or salt pork, diced
1 chopped onion
1 chopped celery stalk, keeping the leaves (alternatively,
    substitute two leeks for the onion and celery)
180 ml water or stock or white wine
650 g potatoes chopped into small cubes
1 bay leaf
Sprig thyme
Level tsp salt
Black pepper
360 ml single cream
3 tbsp butter
280 g can baby clams in juice
Baguette

Preparation

....

1. Fry the bacon pieces in large saucepan on medium heat for 5 minutes until they start to crisp, add onions and celery and cook for another 5 minutes.

2. Add water, wine or stock and potatoes, half the clam liquid, herbs, salt and pepper. Bring to simmer and cook uncovered for another 15 minutes or until potatoes are tender.

3. Stir in the cream, half the butter and the clams, and cook on a gentle heat until thick, not allowing the soup to boil. For a thicker soup, blend 1 tbsp flour into the cream before adding.

4. Allow the soup to sit for a while, and re-heat to a simmer when ready to serve.

5. In the absence of ship biscuits, stir-fry cubes of baguette in the rest of the butter for a few minutes to make croutons. Salted crackers make a great alternative.

6. Pour the soup into bowls, sprinkle croutons on top and garnish with chopped celery leaves and more black pepper.

Pork: Salted, Smoked or Cured

In Europe, smoked or cured pork – ham or bacon – kept well in the days before refrigeration, and in a medieval peasant household (as in *Gammer Gurton's Needle* – see p.80) it would be hung up to keep the rats away, in much the way hams are still hung from the rafters in Spain today.

Salt pork is made from the same cuts as bacon, but saltier, and isn't cured or smoked. Because it kept for a long time, it was used on long sea journeys, hence its inclusion in New England clam chowder. It also found its way into much traditional American home cooking, sometimes paired with beans in the Boston area or with greens further south. In *To Kill a Mockingbird* by Harper Lee, the kitchen table is loaded with 'enough food to bury the family: hunks of salt pork, tomatoes, beans, even scuppernongs'.

For lunch I ate the kipper fillets... garnished with lemon juice, oil, and a light sprinkling of dry herbs.

The Sea, the Sea, Iris Murdoch

MARINATED KIPPERS

Charles Arrowby, the narrator of the novel, is a theatre director who has retired to a house by the sea to write his memoirs. He describes his lunches quite obsessively and yet they often sound hilariously unappealing, such as his tinned macaroni 'jazzed up' with oil, garlic and more cheese. The kippers sound all right, except for the dry herbs and the tinned new potatoes he serves them with.

Serves 2

Ingredients

1 kipper	1 tbsp olive oil
1 shallot	Zest of ½ a lemon
1 tsp fresh dill	1 tsp malt vinegar
1 tsp fresh parsley	Salt and pepper

Preparation

1. The kipper should be skinned and boned first. Ask your fishmonger to do this for you.

2. To make the marinade, first chop the shallot finely, then chop the dill and parsley and add them to a bowl.

3. Mix in the olive oil, lemon zest and vinegar with the shallot and herbs, and season with salt and pepper to taste; cover the kipper fillet well with the marinade and chill overnight.

4. Halve the kipper and serve with bread or potato salad.

The piles of vegetables on the pavement now extended to the verge of the roadway. Between the heaps, the market gardeners left narrow paths to enable people to pass along. The whole of the wide footway was covered from end to end with dark mounds. As yet, in the sudden dancing gleams of light from the lanterns, you only just espied the luxuriant fullness of the bundles of artichokes, the delicate green of the lettuces, the rosy coral of the carrots, the dull ivory of the turnips. And these gleams of rich colour flitted along the heaps, according as the lanterns came and went... In the distance a loud voice could be heard crying, 'Endive! who's got endive?'

The Fat and the Thin, or *The Belly of Paris*, Émile Zola

ENDIVES AND ORANGES

This French novel is set around Les Halles, the great market in the centre of Paris during the nineteenth century. The Fat and the Thin refers to the bourgeois and the working class, as the former are taking over the city. The vivid hues of this scene make me want to eat something colourful and fresh. The main character is caught up in intriguing events concerning market vendors including a cheese seller – so I'll include some French cheese in this recipe.

Serves 4

Ingredients

....

3 oranges (including if possible 1 blood orange)
2 heads endive
Small piece of crumbly blue cheese such as bleu d'Auvergne
    or Roquefort
50 g toasted sliced almonds
Coarse salt and ground pepper
Olive oil
Cider vinegar or balsamic

Preparation

1. Cut the peel and any white insides off the oranges, and chop the flesh into small, colourful pieces.

2. Trim the ends of the endives, separate the leaves and arrange them on a large plate.

3. Crumble the blue cheese into small pieces lightly with your fingers.

4. Fill the boat-shaped endive leaves with pieces of orange, blue cheese and almonds, then season with salt and pepper and drizzle with olive oil and vinegar.

He liked thick giblet soup, nutty gizzards, a stuffed roast heart, liver slices fried with crustcrumbs, fried hencods' roes.

Ulysses, James Joyce

LIVER SLICES IN CRUSTCRUMBS FOR LEOPOLD BLOOM

Leopold Bloom has a lusty appetite and, as we follow him around Dublin for a day, we learn that he's even partial to a nice sheep's trotter or a pig's foot. While such tastes may not tantalise every reader, crumbed slices of liver are more easily palatable. Eat on 16 June, Bloomsday.

Serves 4

Ingredients

4 thin slices calves' liver
150 g breadcrumbs
4 slices smoked bacon
2 onions, thinly sliced

1 apple, thinly sliced
½ glass white wine
1 tbsp butter
1 tbsp cooking oil

Preparation

1. Ideally the liver should be sliced very thin, a quarter of an inch; which is best done by a butcher. Otherwise – it will be hard to slice it so thinly at home – you will have to cook for a little longer than a few minutes until it's tender and brown.

2. Press liver slices into breadcrumbs and set aside.

3. Brown the bacon in a frying pan, without crisping it, set aside on a plate and keep warm.

4. Fry the onion in the bacon fat until soft, add apple slices and cook for a few minutes, then add the wine and cook until the apple is soft.

5. Arrange the onion and apple on a plate with the bacon.

6. Heat the butter and oil in the pan, and fry the liver on both sides for a few minutes on a medium heat until tender, brown on the outside but still a little pink inside, then lay over the bacon, apple and onions.

Odes to Offal

James Joyce's Leopold Bloom is literature's most famous offal-eater, eating with relish 'the inner organs of beasts and fowls' including those famous mutton kidneys with the 'fine tang of faintly scented urine'.

There is, however, an intensely memorable scene in *Burial Rites* by Australian author Hannah Kent, shortlisted for *The Guardian* First Book Award. In 1830, in Iceland, Agnes awaits her sentence for murder on an isolated farm. The book is full of references to food, from the churning of butter to the making of blood sausage with suet, rye flour and lichen in a smoky kitchen, when 'the croft is thick with the animal smell of boiling fat and kidneys, frying for the men's breakfast'.

'A loaf of bread,' the Walrus said,
'Is what we chiefly need:
Pepper and vinegar besides
Are very good indeed –
Now if you're ready, Oysters dear,
We can begin to feed.'
'But not on us!' the Oysters cried,
Turning a little blue.
'After such kindness, that would be
A dismal thing to do!'
'The night is fine,' the Walrus said.
'Do you admire the view?

From 'The Walrus and the Carpenter', Lewis Carroll

WALRUS AND CARPENTER OYSTERS

The classic recipe can't be much improved upon: plenty of fresh, young, gullible oysters. Walruses like fat ones, but your guests may prefer medium-sized; shuck them with an oyster knife, or ask your fishmonger to do it for you.

Serves 6

Ingredients

....

Oysters (at least 4 per
   person)
Loaf of bread

Butter
Pepper
Rice wine vinegar

Preparation

....

1. Take your time to talk of many things – shoes and ships and sealing wax, cabbages and kings. Don't spread the butter too thick. A pocket handkerchief may be useful. Serve in the middle of the night, with the sun shining on the sea.

2. Half-fill a small bowl with vinegar, and add a smidgeon of grated, peeled fresh ginger, finely chopped small red chilli (deseeded) and a squeeze of lime juice.

3. Spoon the dressing onto the flesh of the oyster, pick up the shell and tip the flesh into your mouth – chewing or simply swallowing.

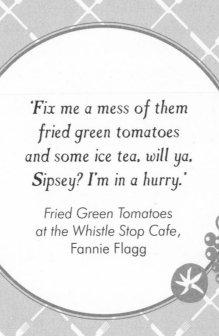

'Fix me a mess of them fried green tomatoes and some ice tea, will ya, Sipsey? I'm in a hurry.'

Fried Green Tomatoes at the Whistle Stop Cafe, Fannie Flagg

FRIED GREEN TOMATOES FOR FOLKS TO REMEMBER

The Whistle Stop Cafe was based on a real cafe near where Fannie Flagg was born in Irondale, Alabama, specialising in fried green tomatoes of course. It was run by her great-aunt Bess in the 1930s. But it was the Hollywood effect, when the book was adapted and released as a film in 1992, that gave the dish its Southern association. The first recorded recipe is actually from a Chicago newspaper in 1877 and it became a standard way of using up unripe tomatoes from your kitchen garden.

Serves 8

Ingredients

8 large green tomatoes
240 g plain flour
4 eggs
240 ml milk
150 g cornmeal
150 g breadcrumbs
Salt and ground black pepper
Cayenne and paprika
1 litre cooking oil

For the dipping sauce:
180 ml mayonnaise
Generous handful fresh basil leaves
1 tbsp lemon juice
1 tsp lemon zest

Preparation

1. First make your basil dipping sauce by whizzing the mayonnaise, basil leaves and lemon juice in a food processor. Season to taste, and refrigerate.

2. Slice the tomatoes 1 cm thick, discarding the ends, and season with salt and black pepper.

3. Spread the flour on a plate.

4. In a bowl, whisk the eggs and milk.

5. Mix cornmeal, breadcrumbs, cayenne and paprika in a bowl.

6. Dip the tomato slices first in the flour, then in the egg mix, then in the breadcrumbs, coating them thoroughly.

7. Pour oil into a heavy frying pan until no less than 1 cm deep and, when at a medium heat, place the tomato slices into the oil in batches, allowing them space in the pan so the slices aren't touching.

8. Flip them once to brown on both sides, about 2 to 3 minutes each side, then drain on paper towels.

ALGERNON [Picking up empty plate in horror]: Good heavens! Lane! Why are there no cucumber sandwiches? I ordered them specially.

LANE [Gravely]: There were no cucumbers in the market this morning, sir. I went down twice.

ALGERNON: No cucumbers!

LANE: No, sir. Not even for ready money.

ALGERNON: That will do, Lane, thank you.

LANE: Thank you, sir. [Goes out]

ALGERNON: I am greatly distressed, Aunt Augusta, about there being no cucumbers, not even for ready money.

LADY BRACKNELL: It really makes no matter, Algernon. I had some crumpets with Lady Harbury, who seems to me to be living entirely for pleasure now.

ALGERNON: I hear her hair has turned quite gold from grief.

The Importance of Being Earnest, Oscar Wilde

THE IMPORTANCE OF CUCUMBER SANDWICHES

If you're opting for Lady Bracknell-style dainty sandwiches, you can use a cookie-cutter to cut sliced white bread into rounds just big enough for one slice of cucumber each. Instead of the cream cheese mixture you can use unsalted butter.

Serves 4

Ingredients

1 cucumber
150 g cream cheese
1 heaped tbsp chopped dill
Juice of ½ lemon
8 slices bread – a springy, soft loaf, not too chewy or crusty
Salt and pepper

Preparation

1. If you want to be traditional, remove the cucumber skin using a potato peeler; or peel off half the skin in lengthwise stripes to keep some flavour. Of course it is perfectly fine to keep the skin on, as long as you're not serving them at a Lady Bracknell-style tea.

2. Slice the cucumber into very thin rounds, and place between paper towels in a colander to drain for 10 minutes.

3. Combine the cream cheese with the dill and lemon juice.

4. Slice the bread approximately 1 cm thick, and spread with cream cheese mixture.

5. Arrange the cucumber slices, overlapping slightly on top, and sprinkle with rock salt and freshly ground black pepper.

'There's cold chicken inside it,' replied the Rat briefly; 'coldtonguecoldhamcoldbeef-pickledgherkinsaladfrenchrollscresssandwiches-pottedmeatgingerbeerlemonadesodawater–'

'O stop, stop,' cried the Mole in ecstasies: 'This is too much!'

'Do you really think so?' enquired the Rat seriously. 'It's only what I always take on these little excursions; and the other animals are always telling me that I'm a mean beast and cut it VERY fine!'

The Wind in the Willows, Kenneth Grahame

COLD BEEF PICNIC SANDWICHES

*A perfect way to use up the beef from
the previous night's roast.*

Serves 2

Ingredients

....

Cold roast beef
4 onion bread rolls
Handful of watercress
½ red onion
Mustard and/or horseradish sauce

Preparation

....

1. Mmm, cold roast beef: don't be a mean beast – cut a few slices per roll.

2. Layer the beef onto the rolls with a couple of sprigs of watercress, a thin slice of red onion and a dash of mustard or horseradish per roll for a satisfying snack – one that's not *too* much.

> The proper way to eat a fig, in society,
> Is to split it in four, holding it by the stump,
> And open it, so that it is a glittering, rosy, moist,
> honied, heavy-petalled four-petalled flower.
>
> Then you throw away the skin
> Which is just like a four-sepalled calyx,
> After you have taken off the blossom, with your lips.
>
> But the vulgar way
> Is just to put your mouth to the crack,
> and take out the flesh in one bite.
>
> Every fruit has its secret.

From 'Figs', D. H. Lawrence

FIGS THE PROPER WAY

*Fresh figs are delicious eaten any way, the riper the better:
picked straight from the tree on a summer's day is my
favourite. A classic combination is with goat's cheese, however,
if the figs have been transported a long way from picking,
they do benefit from a little baking to bring out the flavour.*

Serves 4

Ingredients

....

4 fresh large figs
100 g goat's cheese
8 slices Parma ham
Baby salad leaves
Olive oil and balsamic vinegar for dressing
Optional:
1 tbsp piquant honey or maple syrup

Preparation

....

1. Heat the oven to 220°C.

2. Cut the stalk ends off the figs, and cut a cross on top (as
    you would Brussels sprouts).

3. Break the goat's cheese into quarters, and gently stuff each fig with a piece.

4. Wrap the ham around each stuffed fig to seal in the cheese, place on a baking sheet and bake for approximately 8 minutes, or until the cheese is melted and the ham crisp.

5. In the meantime, dress the salad with the oil and vinegar and arrange in bowls, ready for the figs.

6. If you have a good piquant honey or real maple syrup, add a drizzle on top.

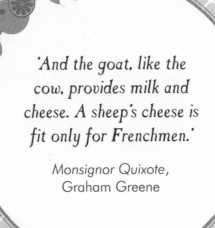

'And the goat, like the cow, provides milk and cheese. A sheep's cheese is fit only for Frenchmen.'

Monsignor Quixote,
Graham Greene

COURGETTE FRITTATA WITH SHEEP'S CHEESE

*On their journey through post-Franco Spain in Greene's
pastiche of the Cervantes novel, the priest Quixote and
the communist ex-mayor Sancho spend many a happy
hour eating, drinking and having lively discussions by the
roadside. While their picnics are basic, they could easily have
encountered this Spanish tortilla-style dish at a local hostelry.*

Serves 4

Ingredients

....

3 tbsp olive oil
2 large courgettes, grated
2 garlic cloves, peeled and finely minced
Splash of white wine
1 tbsp fresh sage leaves, finely chopped (parsley and dill also
   work well – whatever you have fresh)
1 tbsp butter
5 eggs
Coarse salt and fresh ground black pepper
70 g soft sheep's milk cheese

Preparation

....

1. Pour 2 tbsp of the oil into a frying pan and over a low heat fry the courgette and garlic, adding the white wine and stirring, for about 20 minutes.

2. Add sage and butter, mix in and cook for another 3 minutes, then remove from the heat and let it cool.

3. Whisk the eggs, seasoning with salt and pepper.

4. When the courgette mash has cooled, mix it in with the eggs.

5. Heat the rest of the oil in the frying pan. Add half the egg mix to the pan, spread the sheep's cheese evenly all over, then add the rest of the egg mix.

6. Allow to cook until beginning to set. Then to finish it off, you can flip it onto a plate like a Spanish tortilla, or put it under a preheated grill for about 5 minutes until set and golden.

Mussels that are mild and smoky, slender strips of carrot and beet that taste of fennel and olive oil.

The Time Traveler's Wife,
Audrey Niffenegger

CARROT AND BEETROOT TASTING OF FENNEL AND OLIVE OIL

*This delicate salad is one of the antipasti brought
by Lourdes for Henry's forty-third birthday feast,
and eaten accompanied by Sauvignon Blanc.*

Serves 4

Ingredients

2 tsp fennel seeds
60 ml olive oil
3 tbsp lemon juice
2 shallots, finely chopped
1 tsp salt
½ tsp sugar
4 carrots
4 small beetroot

Preparation

1. Toast the fennel seeds until fragrant in a dry frying pan
    over a medium heat, stirring to prevent them from burning.
    Grind them in a pestle and mortar and then place in a
    small bowl or cup and combine with the olive oil.

2. Leave to infuse for 15 minutes.

3. In a bowl, mix the lemon juice, shallots, salt and sugar. Mix with the fennel oil to complete the vinaigrette.

4. Shred the carrots and beetroot into fine strips using a food processor or grater, toss in the dressing and arrange exquisitely on separate plates.

MAINS

To skip to Desserts and Sweets, go to p.155

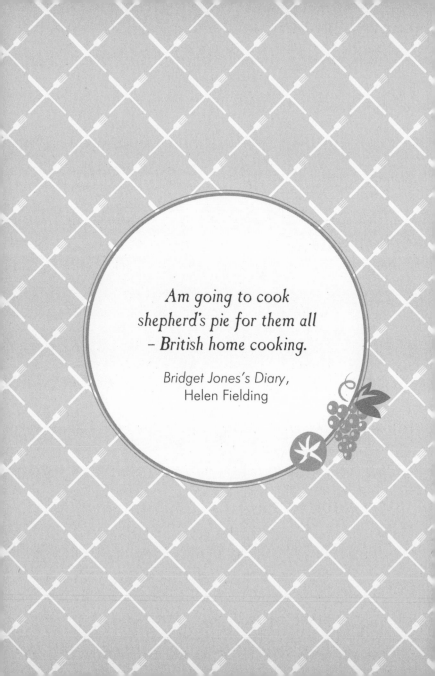

*Am going to cook
shepherd's pie for them all
– British home cooking.*

Bridget Jones's Diary,
Helen Fielding

SHEPHERD'S PIE

How can she mess up shepherd's pie? But dear Bridget can. Preparation for her birthday-party dinner starts to go wrong when she starts sipping on the Grand Marnier meant for the soufflés. She leaves the bag of ingredients for the salad in the shop, and steps in the pan of mashed potatoes in her new kitten heels. When her guests arrive, they tell her to go and get ready while they clean up the kitchen. Then they throw it all away, and go out for dinner instead.

Serves 4

Ingredients

....

1 tbsp olive oil
1 onion, finely chopped
1 carrot, finely diced
2 sticks celery, chopped
500 g minced lamb
1 tbsp flour
240 ml stock
1 tin chopped tomatoes
1 bay leaf or sprig of rosemary
1 tbsp Worcestershire sauce
Mashed potatoes (see p.143 – double the ingredients)

Preparation

....

1. Heat the oil over a medium heat in a frying pan, adding first the onion, celery and carrot for 5 minutes, and then the meat until it starts to brown.

2. Stir in the flour, then slowly add the stock a little at a time, stirring, finally adding the Worcestershire sauce, herbs and chopped tomatoes.

3. Turn down the heat and simmer for 30 minutes, adding salt and pepper to taste.

4. Prepare the mashed potatoes.

5. Add the lamb mixture to an ovenproof dish, then top with the mashed potato and smooth over into peaks with a fork.

6. Bake in the oven for about 20 minutes.

7. If that sounds awfully complicated, go out to the pub instead.

With-oute bake mete was never his hous,
Of fish and flesh, and that so plentevous,
It snewed in his hous of mete and drinke,
Of alle deyntees that men coude thinke.
After the sondry sesons of the yeer,
So chaunged he his mete and his soper.
Ful many a fat partrich hadde he in mewe,
And many a breem and many a luce in stewe.
Wo was his cook, but-if his sauce were
Poynaunt and sharp, and redy al his gere.

───※─────※※※─────※───

Without baked food never was his house,
With fish and flesh, and that so plenteous,
It snowed in his house with meat and drink,
With all the delicacies of which you could think.
After the different seasons of the year,
So he varied his food and his supper.
Many a fat partridge he kept in a cage,
And many a bream and a pike in a pond.
Woe betide his cook unless the sauce were
Piquant and sharp, and his utensils at the ready.

The Canterbury Tales, Geoffrey Chaucer

FAT PARTRIDGE FOR THE FRANKLIN, EPICURUS' OWN SON

October and November are said to be the best months
for eating this delicious gamebird, although Chaucer's
Franklin, whom he describes as 'Epicurus owne sone',
keeps them in a cage to fatten them up and eat them
whenever he likes. Since he liked baked food with
piquant sauces, I think he would have enjoyed this.

Serves 4

Ingredients

300 g potatoes
3 carrots
2 parsnips
½ small pumpkin, deseeded
2 tbsp olive oil
Salt and freshly ground black pepper
4 oven-ready partridges
100 g butter
4 sprigs fresh thyme
12 juniper berries
1 glass red wine
1 glass stock

Preparation

....

1. Cut the vegetables into evenly-sized pieces (the potatoes will likely be in quarters or smaller). Place in a baking tray, add the olive oil and a little of the butter, some salt and pepper, mix together and place in the oven at 200°C for 25 minutes.

2. Add salt and pepper seasoning to the partridges both inside and out, rub with butter, put a sprig of thyme and 3 juniper berries inside each bird and tie the legs with string.

3. Place the partridges in a roasting tray. Stir and turn the vegetables, and place the partridges in the oven alongside.

4. Cook for 30 minutes, basting the partridges with butter from time to time. To check they are cooked, puncture with a skewer between leg and breast – the juices should run clear.

5. Allow the partridges to rest for 10 minutes before serving. In the meantime, pour the meat juices into a saucepan, add wine and stock and simmer to make a gravy to pour over each serving.

My mother... started to buy in huge tins of beans and frankfurter sausages. 'An army marches on its stomach.'

Oranges Are Not the Only Fruit,
Jeanette Winterson

BEANS AND FRANKFURTERS

*Buy the best quality beans and frankfurters you can.
Jeanette Winterson – whose Oranges Are Not the Only
Fruit is a novel based on her own upbringing – ate a lot
of tinned beans and frankfurters as a child, but later as a
successful author bought a house near Spitalfields Market
in London, that was once the offices of an oranges importer
called J. W. Fruits, and opened her own food shop and
cafe, Verde, selling quality, organic and ethical produce.*

Serves 4

Ingredients

Cooking oil
1 large onion

2 large tins baked beans
1 tin frankfurters

Preparation

1. Chop the onion.

2. Heat the oil in a large, deep frying pan, and sauté the
   onion until tender and browning.

3. Add the frankfurters, cut into short pieces, and the beans,
   and cook through.

4. Feed to your own small army.

HODGE: Gog's bread, Diccon, ich
came too late, was nothing there to get!
Gib (a foul fiend might on her light!)
    licked the milk-pan so clean,
See, Diccon, 'twas not so well washed
    this seven year, as ich ween!
A pestilence light on all ill-luck!
    Chad thought, yet for all this
Of a morsel of bacon behind the door
    at worst should not miss:
But when ich sought a slip to cut,
    as ich was wont to do,
Gog's souls, Diccon! Gib, our cat,
    had eat the bacon too!
[*Which bacon Diccon stole, as is declared before.*]
DICCON: Ill-luck, quod he! Marry, swear it,
    Hodge! This day, the truth tell,
Thou rose not on thy right side,
    or else blessed thee not well.
Thy milk slopped up! Thy bacon filched!
    That was too bad luck, Hodge!

Gammer Gurton's Needle, Anonymous

BACON, MUSHROOM AND BLACK PUDDING SALAD IF YOU GOT OUT OF BED ON THE WRONG SIDE

Hodge could quite easily have gathered some mushrooms and greens, and added blood sausage to make this hearty dish – if his bacon hadn't been filched.

Serves 2

Ingredients

....

4 slices of bacon, chopped
6 slices of black pudding
8 large mushrooms, chopped
1 lettuce, washed (or you can substitute red-leaf, frisee, mixed
    leaves or even fresh spinach)
3 tbsp olive oil
1 tbsp balsamic vinegar
Parsley, chopped
Black pepper

Preparation

....

1. Fry the black pudding, bacon and mushrooms in the oil until cooked through.

2.   Take out the ingredients and arrange on top of the salad.

3.   Pour vinegar into the frying pan to deglaze, absorbing the juices, and pour on top of the salad, adding a little oil if more dressing is needed according to taste.

4.   Sprinkle with parsley and ground black pepper.

HAMLET: Thrift, thrift, Horatio! The funeral baked meats Did coldly furnish forth the marriage tables.

Hamlet, William Shakespeare

ROAST PORK OPEN SANDWICHES

*Keeping leftovers from a funeral might seem in poor taste,
but Hamlet is making the point – in one of the play's best-
known lines – that his mother remarried rather hastily after his
father's death. Still, what do you do with your baked meats
the next day? Slices of roast beef, lamb, turkey or pork make
excellent sandwiches, of course; since Hamlet was Prince
of Denmark, it would most likely have been a pork roast.*

Serves 1

Ingredients

Danish rye bread or black bread
Butter
Leftover roast pork, thinly sliced, with crispy crackling
Marinated or pickled red cabbage
½ orange, cut into slices

Preparation

1. Lay out several slices of thin rye bread, and spread
    generously with butter.

2. Pile them with slices of roast pork.

3. Top each with a spoonful of red cabbage and two small
    slices of orange – arrange to look like the horns on a
    Viking helmet.

"

Dickon made the stimulating discovery that in the wood in the park outside the garden where Mary had first found him piping to the wild creatures there was a deep little hollow where you could build a sort of tiny oven with stones and roast potatoes and eggs in it. Roasted eggs were a previously unknown luxury and very hot potatoes with salt and fresh butter in them were fit for a woodland king – besides being deliciously satisfying.

The Secret Garden, Frances Hodgson Burnett

"

ROASTED POTATOES
AND BAKED EGGS

While you can almost taste how good those hot potatoes were, it's hard to feel compelled, except for literary authenticity, to roast an egg, since it seems like a lot of work resulting in something that tastes very much like a boiled one (and there's the risk of ending up with what Shakespeare's Touchstone mentions, 'an ill roasted egg, all on one side'). Roasted eggs are an important part of the Jewish Passover tradition, but they're not eaten. While for Dickon with his limited kitchen facilities, roasting eggs was a luxury, I recommend baking them this way instead.

Serves 2

Ingredients

....

300 g small new potatoes
2 garlic cloves
2 tbsp olive oil
Coarse salt and ground black pepper
Small bunch asparagus
2 small tomatoes
1 courgette
4 eggs
Handful grated cheese

Preparation

....

1. Preheat the oven to 190°C.

2. Crush the garlic cloves with the side of a knife and toss with the potatoes in a large baking dish in olive oil, salt and pepper, then place in the oven and roast for 30 minutes.

3. Discard the woody ends of the asparagus and cut the spears into pieces 3–4 cm long.

4. Halve the tomatoes and slice the courgette, then add all the vegetables to the potatoes in the dish, toss in the oil and continue to roast for another 15 minutes until they are tender.

5. Remove the dish from the oven and make four holes for the eggs.

6. Break an egg into each hole and return to the oven for about 3 minutes until each one is beginning to set but still runny.

7. Grind some black pepper over the top and sprinkle with cheese, return to the oven for 2 minutes then serve immediately.

It is the fair acceptance, sir, creates
The entertainment perfect, not the cates.
Yet shall you have, to rectify your palate,
An olive, capers, or some better salad
Ushering the mutton; with a short-legged hen,
If we can get her, full of eggs, and then
Lemons, and wine for sauce; to these a cony
Is not to be despaired of, for our money;
And, though fowl now be scarce, yet there are clerks,
The sky not falling, think we may have larks.
I'll tell you of more, and lie, so you will come.

From 'Inviting a Friend to Supper', Ben Jonson

CHICKEN WITH CAPERS, LEMON AND WINE

Ben Jonson's imagination conjured a cornucopia of flavours. This dish brings together just a few of them in a fine, light supper that may be enough to lure a friend to dinner without the need to lie about larks.

Serves 2

Ingredients

2 skinless chicken breasts
60 g plain flour
1 tsp salt
1 tbsp cooking oil
½ tbsp butter
2 cloves garlic, minced

½ cup white wine
Juice of 1 small lemon or ½ a large lemon
1 tbsp capers
4 artichoke hearts, quartered
Sprigs parsley

Preparation

1. Mix the flour with the salt on a plate, and dredge the chicken breasts in it until loosely covered.

2. Heat the oil in a heavy frying pan, and add half the butter and allow to melt.

3. Brown the chicken on one side in the pan for about 5 minutes, reduce the heat, turn the chicken over and fry on the other side until cooked through (the inside should be white and firm).

4. Remove the chicken from the pan and set aside on a warm plate. Do not clean the frying pan, and with the pan on a low to medium heat, cook the garlic for a few minutes.

5. Add the white wine and the lemon juice, allow to bubble then simmer for a few minutes, mixing everything well with a wooden spoon, reducing the mixture.

6. Add the rest of the butter, stirring vigorously and keeping the sauce moving so that it doesn't separate.

7. Remove from the heat, add the capers and artichoke hearts, then pour the sauce over the chicken.

8. Serve with pasta, rice or potatoes, and garnish with parsley.

Everything depended upon things being served up the precise moment they were ready. The beef, the bay leaf, and the wine – all must be done to a turn. To keep it waiting was out of the question...

An exquisite scent of olives and oil and juice rose from the great brown dish as Marthe, with a little flourish, took the cover off. The cook had spent three days over that dish. And she must take great care, Mrs Ramsay thought, diving into the soft mass, to choose a specially tender piece for William Bankes. And she peered into the dish, with its shiny walls and its confusion of savoury brown and yellow meats, and its bay leaves and its wine...

'It is a triumph,' said Mr Bankes, laying his knife down for a moment. He had eaten attentively. It was rich. It was tender. It was perfectly cooked.

To the Lighthouse, Virginia Woolf

BOEUF EN DAUBE

Although this is traditionally cooked for a long time to tenderise the meat, you'll be pleased to hear it doesn't necessarily require three days. However, if you would like the boeuf en daube to take at least two days, you may marinate the meat in the herbs and wine overnight; this reduces the time needed for cooking, though.

Serves 6

Ingredients

....

150 g unsmoked streaky bacon or pancetta
Olive oil
1 large onion
1 large carrot
Few pieces of orange zest and 2 tbsp juice of the orange
2 sprigs thyme, 2 bay leaves, 2 cloves
1.5 kg stewing beef (e.g. cheek, shin)
4 cloves garlic
Coarse salt, black peppercorns
Bottle of robust red wine, e.g. Côtes du Rhône or Shiraz
100 g flour
Handful black olives

Preparation

....

1. Remove the rind from the bacon and set aside. Cut the bacon into 2-cm pieces.

2. Pour 3–4 tablespoons olive oil into a large casserole dish and scatter in the bacon pieces. Slice the onion and carrot and lay on top, with the herbs and orange peel.

3. Cut the meat into large chunks and place over the other ingredients.

4. Cut the garlic cloves into a few pieces and place in between the pieces of meat, add salt and pepper.

5. Cut the bacon rind into small pieces and sprinkle on top. Bring the wine to boil in a saucepan and pour over.

6. Mix the flour with 3 tbsp water to form a dough, then roll out to form a long sausage. Coil it around the rim of the casserole dish and press down with the lid, sealing the dish well.

7. In a 90°C oven, cook overnight for 12 hours.

8. Chip at the seal to break open the pot, discarding the pastry. The meat should be tender and the sauce dark. Add in the olives, replace the lid and present to the mistress of the house so she can take all the credit.

A Woolf-ish Appetite

The literary world seems divided on the topic of Virginia Woolf and food. This is the author who wrote, in her essay *A Room of One's Own*: 'One cannot think well, love well, sleep well, if one has not dined well.' Yet others argue there are few references to food in her novels and put this down to the fact that she battled with anorexia throughout her life.

While her scene of boeuf en daube is a favourite passage in her 1927 book, it has been pointed out that it's not an accurate description of the dish of that name. The suggestion that things must be served up 'the precise moment they were ready' is completely untrue: if your guests are late or you chatter away over an aperitif, the boeuf en daube won't come to any harm. Regarding the 'yellow meats' mentioned in the dish, some have pointed out that pot au feu at the time included chicken, but surely boeuf en daube is, well, boeuf?

My theory, however, is that Woolf knew precisely how silly it was to suggest a bay leaf must be done to a turn, and was trying to show Mrs Ramsay's ignorance of cooking, since it was all done by Marthe the maid.

He found Miss Bradwardine presiding over the tea and coffee, the table loaded with warm bread, both of flour, oatmeal, and barleymeal, in the shape of loaves, cakes, biscuits, and other varieties, together with eggs, reindeer ham, mutton and beef ditto, smoked salmon, marmalade, and all the other delicacies which induced even Johnson himself to extol the luxury of a Scotch breakfast above that of all other countries. A mess of oatmeal porridge, flanked by a silver jug, which held an equal mixture of cream and buttermilk, was placed for the Baron's share of this repast.

Waverley, Walter Scott

SCOTCH PANCAKES
WITH SMOKED SALMON

*Reproducing the whole of Waverley's Scottish breakfast
– including the unusual reindeer ham – might seem a
little excessive, but Scotch pancakes with smoked salmon
(Scottish, of course) will conjure the spirit of the occasion.*

Serves 4

Ingredients

....

For the topping:
50 ml crème fraiche
1 tbsp horseradish sauce
1 tsp lemon juice
1 tbsp chopped dill
300 g smoked salmon

For the pancakes:
4 medium potatoes, peeled
    and quartered
75 ml milk
2 eggs
1 tbsp buttermilk
50 g plain flour
Cooking oil

Preparation

....

1. Mix the horseradish, lemon and dill into the crème fraiche
    in a serving bowl, and set to one side.

2. Lay the smoked salmon out separately on serving plates.

3. To make the pancakes, first boil the potatoes until tender, drain and mash, mixing in the milk. Set aside until cool.

4. Separate the eggs into two bowls; whisk the egg whites with a pinch of salt and set aside.

5. Beat the yolks with the buttermilk. Mix with the cooled potatoes and then fold in the flour. Stir a spoonful of the whisked egg whites into the potato mix first, then carefully fold in the remaining egg white.

6. Heat the cooking oil in a frying pan and add batter to form pancakes, cooking each one for a couple of minutes until bubbles are forming, then flipping; they should be golden and cooked through.

7. Remove from pan and place on a wire rack.

8. There should be enough batter to make about 12 pancakes so they will need to be made in a few batches, depending on the size of the pan.

9. Arrange the topping, salmon and pancakes on a table, ready for your guests to help themselves.

There never was such a goose. Bob said he didn't believe there ever was such a goose cooked. Its tenderness and flavour, size and cheapness, were the themes of universal admiration. Eked out by apple sauce and mashed potatoes, it was a sufficient dinner for the whole family; indeed, as Mrs Cratchit said with great delight (surveying one small atom of a bone upon the dish), they hadn't ate it all at last! Yet every one had had enough, and the youngest Cratchits, in particular, were steeped in sage and onion to the eyebrows!

A Christmas Carol, Charles Dickens

ROAST GOOSE WITH SAGE AND ONION

Victorian England was fond of cookbooks, and cooking practices have changed little since Dickens' time. This recipe draws on Mrs Beeton and other contemporary sources, with a few additional touches. When it comes to goose, the cooking is simple: roast it. The main thing to be aware of is the amount of fat that will need to drain off (which of course can be used for roasting potatoes and vegetables, or cooking winter greens).

Serves 4–6

Ingredients

....

1 goose of around 5 kg (thawed if frozen)
Salt and pepper
4 tbsp butter
4 onions, chopped
1 goose liver, reserved from giblets
480 g crumbs from stale bread
Handful fresh sage leaves, chopped
½ cup dry white wine
2 eggs, lightly beaten

Preparation

....

1. Remove the giblets from the goose and reserve the liver, discarding the rest. Clip off its wing tips using kitchen shears, then wash the bird inside and out. Rub salt and pepper inside and out. Set aside while you prepare the stuffing.

2. Preheat the oven to 200°C.

3. Melt 3 tbsp butter in a large saucepan over a medium heat and then cook the onions, stirring, until softened and translucent.

4. Transfer onions to a large mixing bowl. Add the rest of the butter to the pan and cook the goose liver until brown and just cooked through.

5. Chop the liver and add with the butter from the pan to the onions. Lightly mix in the crumbs, sage, 1 tsp salt and pepper each, wine and eggs. Do not wash the pan, as you can use it for the gravy later.

6. When the goose is ready to be cooked, prick the skin all over with a fork, then stuff the neck and belly cavities with the sage and onion mixture. If necessary, you can close up a cavity with stitches or by tying the legs with string.

7. Place the goose breast side up on a rack over a roasting pan, and roast it in the oven for 30 minutes, when you can reduce the heat to 175°C and drain off some of the fat from the dish.

8. Turn goose on its side and roast for 1 hour, basting every 20 minutes.

9. Turn on its other side and roast for 1 hour again, basting again and draining off fat as necessary.

10. Return to breast side up and roast for a final 30 minutes until browned all over.

11. Allow to rest for 10 minutes while making a gravy; some use the wing tips to make juice for the gravy.

What's Good for the Goose

In October 1851, the second edition of a slim, paperback book of menus or 'Bills of Fare' was published in London, called *What Shall We Have For Dinner?* The author purported to be Lady Maria Clutterbuck, widow of Sir Jonas Clutterbuck, 'not a gourmand but a man of great gastronomical experience'; but it later emerged that this was a pseudonym for Catherine Thomson Dickens, wife of Charles. The date of the first edition is not known, but the book must have been popular as it was reissued several times throughout the 1850s. Charles Dickens never mentions it in his letters, though he talks of his large household at London's Devonshire Terrace with nine children, and his wife's poor health and his own books.

The cookbook has two menus built around roast goose, which might have been a Dickens household favourite. She provides

very few vegetable dishes in the book, including potato balls and cauliflower with Parmesan cheese (*A Christmas Carol* itself only mentions potatoes and onions among its lengthy descriptions of food), but suggests serving winter vegetable soup with roast goose.

Goose, fattier and darker than turkey, was favoured for feasts for many centuries; French and German Jewish communities in the Middle Ages fattened their geese in the autumn for Hanukkah. In much of Western Europe, goose was enjoyed at Michaelmas, at the end of September, for the feast of the Archangel Michael. The Pilgrims took the domesticated goose to America and it remained the most popular holiday dish until the nineteenth century. In the story *The Little Match Girl* by Danish author Hans Christian Anderson, published in 1845, on a snow-white tablecloth the roast goose was 'steaming famously'.

The table was laid under the cart-shed. On it were four sirloins, six chicken fricassees, stewed veal, three legs of mutton, and in the middle a fine roast suckling pig, flanked by four chitterlings with sorrel. At the corners were decanters of brandy. Sweet bottled-cider frothed round the corks, and all the glasses had been filled to the brim with wine beforehand. Large dishes of yellow cream, that trembled with the least shake of the table, had designed on their smooth surface the initials of the newly wedded pair in nonpareil arabesques.

Madame Bovary, Gustave Flaubert

CHICKEN FRICASSEE

Recipes for and references to 'friquassee' are found as early as medieval times in the French cookbook Le Viandier. *The term first entered English in the sixteenth century, and it is speculated to be a combination of the words for frying and breaking. Traditionally, the meat is broken into pieces and then sautéed, but not browned. Liquid is then added; traditionally a white sauce. It is said to have been one of Abraham Lincoln's favourite dishes. I'll leave the chitterlings for another time.*

Serves 4

Ingredients

....

2 tbsp cooking oil
1.5 kg chicken pieces
1 tbsp flour
Salt and pepper
100 g finely chopped shallots
1 clove garlic, crushed
½ glass white wine
1 bay leaf
240 ml chicken stock
3 sprigs fresh tarragon
1 egg yolk
1 tbsp cream
Squeeze lemon juice

Preparation

....

1. Heat half the oil in a frying pan on medium to high heat.

2. Coat chicken pieces in flour and add to the pan. Add salt and pepper, and cook until golden (not brown), then remove from pan and set aside.

3. Add the rest of the oil to the pan and cook the shallots and garlic for about 5 minutes until softened.

4. Turn up the heat, add the wine and bay leaf, stir and reduce, then add stock, chicken and tarragon and cook vigorously for a few minutes until bubbling.

5. Reduce the heat and simmer, covered, for about 45 minutes until the meat is tender. Remove chicken to serving plate.

6. Whisk the egg yolk and cream in a bowl, add a little of the hot liquid from the pan to the bowl, then pour into the pan to create a sauce.

7. Add lemon, season to taste, remove the bay leaf then pour over the chicken.

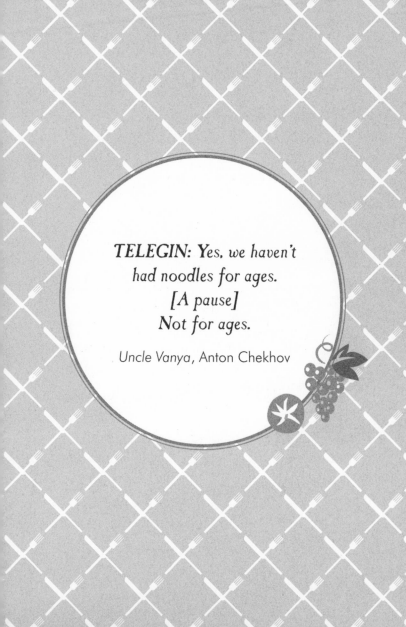

TELEGIN: Yes, we haven't had noodles for ages.
[A pause]
Not for ages.

Uncle Vanya, Anton Chekhov

TRADITIONAL RUSSIAN EGG NOODLES (LAPSHA)

This is a wonderful comfort food. You can understand why Telegin would be wistful.

Serves 8

Ingredients

120 ml water
110 g melted butter
1½ tsp salt
6 large eggs
600 g plain flour
110 g butter for cooking
Sour cream

Preparation

1. Boil the water in a large saucepan, add the butter and allow to melt; whisk together and then allow to cool a little.

2. In a large mixing bowl, beat the eggs with the salt. Slowly add the butter mixture to the eggs, whisking until well blended.

3. Gradually add the flour to the bowl, mixing to form a dough, then knead on a floured surface for 10 minutes.

4. Divide the dough into balls roughly the size of an orange and cover with a damp cloth, allowing to rest for 15 minutes.

5. Using a rolling pin, roll out each ball in turn as thinly as possible. Roll up each sheet of dough like a carpet or a Swiss roll, cut to thin noodles, as thin as possible (if you have a pasta maker, so much the better).

6. Boil water with salt and plenty of butter, drop the noodles in the pot and simmer for about 5 minutes.

7. Ladle into bowls and serve with dollops of sour cream.

Tita was literally 'like water for hot chocolate' – she was on the verge of boiling over.

Like Water for Chocolate,
Laura Esquivel

CHAMPANDONGO

Tita is rushing and in such a bad temper she's on the verge of boiling over when she starts making her champandongo, which would ordinarily suggest the dish wouldn't turn out as delicious. She is in such a hurry she drops the mole sauce down the stairs. But thanks to the essential flavours of champandongo – a dish that can be described as a kind of Mexican lasagne – 'no temper can be bad enough to ruin its enjoyment'.

Serves 4

Ingredients

Cooking oil
4 large flour or corn tortillas
1 onion, finely chopped
250 g minced beef
250 g minced pork
2 tsp cumin
1 tbsp sugar
2 tomatoes, chopped

Juice of 1 orange
200 g walnuts
200 g almonds
60 g mole sauce
240 ml chicken stock
60 ml sour cream
250 g Manchego cheese, sliced

Preparation

1. Heat a little cooking oil in a frying pan and warm the tortillas gently on each side until golden, then set aside on paper towels.

2. Break the walnuts and almonds into small pieces using a pestle and mortar.

3. Fry the onion until translucent, then add the meat, the cumin and sugar. When the meat is beginning to brown, add the tomatoes and orange juice, and then the walnuts and almonds and continue to cook for 5 minutes, stirring.

4. In a saucepan, stir and blend the mole with the chicken stock.

5. The ingredients then get layered into a dish, like a lasagne or moussaka. First spread a layer of sour cream in a glass baking dish, followed by a layer of tortillas, layers of meat mixture and mole, and a layer of cheese, repeating until the dish is filled.

6. Place in an oven, around 180°C, and bake for around 15 minutes until the cheese has melted.

7. Serve with beans.

I hadn't had a bite to eat since yesterday, so Jim he got out some corn-dodgers and buttermilk, and pork and cabbage and greens – there ain't nothing in the world so good when it's cooked right – and whilst I eat my supper we talked and had a good time.

Huckleberry Finn, Mark Twain

PORK AND CABBAGE AND GREENS

Collard greens, as eaten by Huckleberry Finn on the Mississippi, are from the cabbage family, also related to kale. The slaves in the American South were given greens from the plantation kitchens, as well as ham hocks and pigs' feet, and from these simple, cheap ingredients came one of the staples of Southern cooking. The traditional cooking method is to simmer the greens for a long time with a piece of salt pork or ham hock, and serve with fresh cornbread to dip into the juices, known as 'pot-likker'.

Serves 4

Ingredients

....

250 g approx. ham hock or salt pork
1 small chilli pepper, seeds removed
Fresh ground black pepper
½ clove garlic, sliced thinly
Large bunch of collards or other greens
1 tbsp butter

Preparation

1. Fill a large pot two-thirds with water, add meat and chilli pepper, garlic and black pepper. Bring to boil and then reduce heat and cook gently for 1 hour.

2. Clean the collard or other greens, and remove any thick stems. Roughly chop into strips.

3. Add the greens and the butter to the pot, and simmer for another 45 minutes to 1 hour.

4. Serve in a shallow bowl.

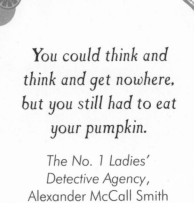

You could think and
think and get nowhere,
but you still had to eat
your pumpkin.

*The No. 1 Ladies'
Detective Agency,*
Alexander McCall Smith

PUMPKIN STEW

Precious Ramotswe's most endearing features include her down-to-earth love of pumpkin and her pragmatism. When she has a complicated problem to solve, then cooking a pot of pumpkin reassures her of the essential simplicity of life and gives her 'a reason for going on'.

Serves 2

Ingredients

....

500 g pumpkin
2 cloves garlic
1 small chilli pepper
1 small onion
2 tbsp cooking oil
½ tsp salt
1 tsp brown sugar
1 tsp ground cumin
1 tsp ground coriander
40 g roasted, unsalted peanuts, crushed
190 g rice

Preparation

....

1.   Peel and cube the pumpkin.

2. Mince the garlic and chilli, and slice the onion.

3. In a large pot, heat the oil and fry the onion and chilli until the onion turns golden, then add the garlic and continue to cook for a few more minutes.

4. Add the pumpkin, salt and sugar, cook and stir, checking the pumpkin doesn't stick to the pan, until it becomes tender enough to mash. Use a wooden spoon to mash it in the pot – you can leave it slightly chunky if you like – and mix in the cumin and coriander.

5. Serve in a bowl with rice, sprinkling peanuts on top, and a mug of bush tea.

He took a slice of bread, an onion and handful of olives. He ate voraciously, tipped up the calabash.

Zorba the Greek,
Nikos Kazantzakis

FISH WITH A MEDITERRANEAN FLAVOUR

*For Nikos Kazantzakis' legendary character Zorba,
a frugal heart is satisfied by a glass of wine, a roast
chestnut and the sound of the sea. He ate as he lived –
voraciously and with love – yet for all the restaurants
named after him, he was happy with simple food.*

Serves 2

Ingredients

Olive oil
1 small onion, sliced
2 cloves garlic, sliced finely
1 tbsp each of fresh basil/parsley, and oregano/thyme,
   less if dried
400 g tin plum tomatoes or passata
Sea salt and fresh ground black pepper
300 g fresh white fish fillets
10–12 juicy black olives
1 tsp capers (caper leaves if available, as used on Crete)
Handful cherry tomatoes, halved

Preparation

1. Heat the olive oil in a frying pan, fry the onion until softened, then add the garlic.

2. Mince the stalks of the fresh herbs and add those, then add the tomatoes.

3. Gradually break up the tomatoes and simmer the sauce for ½ hour, seasoning with the salt and pepper and adding half of the herbs. Preheat the oven to 220°C.

4. Pour the tomato sauce into a baking dish and add the fish fillets. With your fingers, squash the olives and remove the stones, then scatter over with the capers, remaining herbs and cherry tomatoes.

5. Add a touch of olive oil and a couple of grinds of pepper, and place in the oven for 15 minutes or until the fish is white throughout.

6. Serve with bread and wine, and don't forget to dance.

'But my yogi is not a cow,' said Kim, gravely, making a hole with his fingers in the top of the mound. 'A little curry is good, and a fried cake and a morsel of conserve would please him, I think.'

'It is a hole as big as thy head,' said the woman fretfully. But she filled it, none the less, with good, steaming vegetable curry, clapped a dried cake atop, and a morsel of clarified butter on the cake, dabbed a lump of sour tamarind conserve at the side; and Kim looked at the load lovingly.

Kim, Rudyard Kipling

KICHREE

Kichree, or kicharee, means 'mixture' in Hindi, so there are many variations on this simple vegetable dish (see p.125). This plain and wholesome dish can be made spicier in a version called vaghareli kichree, but I love the simplicity of this recipe for a no-fuss, nutritious detox lunch or supper, to savour slowly while reading a good book. If you find it too plain, you can add a little cumin, ground ginger or mustard seed with the turmeric.

Serves 1

Ingredients

50 g green lentils
50 g basmati rice
Pinch salt
½ tsp turmeric

Preparation

1. Leave the rice and lentils to soak for a few hours, then rinse a few times until the water runs clear.

2. Put in a saucepan and cover with water, so the contents is one part lentils and rice, and two parts water.

3. Bring to the boil, add the salt and turmeric, then simmer until tender.

4. This should take around 15 minutes, but check to see if more water is needed so they don't stick to the pot.

5. Serve with a blob of butter melting on top, or a spoonful of yoghurt.

Exceedingly Good Curry

Rudyard Kipling, a recipient of the Nobel Prize for Literature and author of such fantastically popular books for children as *The Jungle Book*, was born in Bombay in 1865. His parents were newly arrived in India, his father (an architect and artist) having come to the colony to preserve the native Indian traditional styles, then threatened by British commercial interests in the country.

Rudyard and his sister loved exploring the local markets with their nanny until he was sent back to Southsea, England, at the age of six for schooling; he hated the home where he was billeted. But those early experiences were to prove a powerful influence. He wrote in later life that his first memories were 'of daybreak, light and colour and golden and purple fruits at the level of my shoulder'.

In *Kim*, he tells the story of a boy whose parents have died, and who continually escapes the house of his guardian, an opium-smoking woman, to find food. His loving descriptions of Indian food were clearly inspired by his own boyhood appetites. He meets people and learns about the country's culture through his searches for food. At one point, in conversation with Hurree Babu, says, 'That is kichree – vegetable curry.' Kichree, made plain or with spices, is a simple comfort food made of rice and legumes, and was the inspiration for the Anglo-Indian invention kedgeree.

When Diana dished the peas she tasted them and a very peculiar expression crossed her face.

'Anne, did YOU put sugar in these peas?'

'Yes,' said Anne, mashing the potatoes with the air of one expected to do her duty. 'I put a spoonful of sugar in. We always do. Don't you like it?'

'But I put a spoonful in too, when I set them on the stove,' said Diana.

Anne dropped her masher and tasted the peas also. Then she made a grimace.

'How awful! I never dreamed you had put sugar in, because I knew your mother never does. I happened to think of it, for a wonder... I'm always forgetting it... so I popped a spoonful in.'

'It's a case of too many cooks, I guess,' said Marilla, who had listened to this dialogue with a rather guilty expression. 'I didn't think you'd remember about the sugar, Anne, for I'm perfectly certain you never did before... so I put in a spoonful.'

The guests in the parlor heard peal after peal of laughter from the kitchen, but they never knew what the fun was about. There were no green peas on the dinner table that day, however.

Anne of Green Gables, Lucy Maud Montgomery

SWEET PEA GNOCCHI

Without sugar, because the peas are sweet enough as they are...

Serves 4

Ingredients

....

400 g peas (fresh or frozen)
400 g potatoes, whole
240 g flour
1 egg, whisked
Salt
Olive oil
50 g fresh Parmesan cheese
Small handful fresh mint, roughly chopped

Optional:
100 g smoked bacon, diced

Preparation

....

1. Bake the potatoes at 180°C for around 45 minutes.

2. Meanwhile, boil the peas and puree them in a large bowl.

3. Remove the potatoes from the oven when cooked through, scoop out the flesh and mash it, adding to the pureed peas. Mix in the flour, egg and a pinch of salt to make a smooth, soft dough.

4. Shape the mixture into gnocchi – tiny rugby balls.

5. Bring a pan of salted water to boil and drop the gnocchi in. As they are done, they will rise to the surface, so scoop them out with a slatted spoon.

6. If using bacon, add to a warm frying pan and stir in the gnocchi. Otherwise, simply serve with a glug of olive oil on top and Parmesan grated over.

7. Decorate with the mint.

George gathered wood and made a fire, and Harris and I started to peel the potatoes. I should never have thought that peeling potatoes was such an undertaking. The job turned out to be the biggest thing of its kind that I had ever been in. We began cheerfully, one might almost say skittishly, but our light-heartedness was gone by the time the first potato was finished. The more we peeled, the more peel there seemed to be left on; by the time we had got all the peel off and all the eyes out, there was no potato left – at least none worth speaking of. George came and had a look at it – it was about the size of a peanut... so we washed half-a-dozen or so more, and put them in without peeling. We also put in a cabbage and about half a peck of peas. George stirred it all up, and then he said that there seemed to be a lot of room to spare, so we overhauled both the hampers, and picked out all the odds and ends and the remnants, and added them to the stew. There were half a pork pie and a bit of cold boiled bacon left, and we put them in. Then George found half a tin of potted salmon, and he emptied that into the pot.

He said that was the advantage of Irish stew: you got rid of such a lot of things.

Three Men in a Boat, Jerome K. Jerome

IRISH STEW

It's hardly surprising that Irish stew, as interpreted by those particular three men in a boat, tastes like 'nothing else on earth'. The more traditional recipe for Irish beef stew is similar to that for boeuf en daube. The difference is that it calls for Guinness as well as wine (the three men would have approved of the beer) and makes good use of Irish root vegetables; it's also very often made with lamb, so that's what I'll use here, for variety.

Serves 6

Ingredients

....

1.5 kg lamb neck chops, cut in half, or lamb shoulder,
   cut in pieces
Cooking oil
3 chopped onions
2 tbsp tomato paste
60 g plain flour
1 pint Guinness
1 beef stock cube
1 kg potatoes, peeled and sliced
2 sliced carrots
Handful frozen peas
Handful chopped fresh parsley to garnish

Preparation

....

1. Trim any excess fat off the meat.

2. Brown the meat in oil in a large pot, then set aside the meat.

3. Add the onions to the pot, fry for a few minutes then add 120 ml of water to remove the brown bits from the bottom of the pan. Add the tomato paste and continue to cook for a few minutes.

4. Put the meat back in the pot, sprinkle the flour over and stir thoroughly. Add a pint of Guinness and a pint of beef stock.

5. Bring to the boil, then turn the heat down, cover and simmer, stirring occasionally and adding more water if necessary.

6. After 1 hour and 20 minutes, add the potatoes and the carrots, and continue cooking for another 30 minutes until the vegetables are tender.

7. Then add a handful of frozen peas and when they are cooked through, it's ready to serve with the parsley garnish.

Silverton was in a mood of titanic pessimism. How any one could come to such a damned hole as the Riviera – any one with a grain of imagination – with the whole Mediterranean to choose from: but then, if one's estimate of a place depended on the way they broiled a spring chicken! Gad!

The House of Mirth, Edith Wharton

MEDITERRANEAN CHICKEN

While American poet Ned Silverton is disgruntled with the Promenade des Anglais, despite its reputation of serving delicious chicken (an important factor of any sojourn), it seems he should be a little more preoccupied with the scandal and infidelities that pervade his social circles. If he had tasted this dish while there, it might have put him in a better mood.

Serves 1

Ingredients

....

2 tbsp olive oil
1 crushed garlic clove
1 tsp oregano
½ tsp sea salt, ½ tsp ground black pepper
1 medium aubergine, sliced lengthways
Favourite cut of chicken for 1, chopped into small pieces
1 small can white beans
Handful cherry tomatoes

Preparation

....

1. Mix the olive oil with the garlic, herbs, salt and pepper.

2. Spread the oil and herbs in a medium-sized baking dish and lay 1-cm slices of aubergine inside it and add more oil, ensuring all the aubergine is covered.

3. Place in the oven at 220°C and roast for 10 minutes. Meanwhile, press the chicken pieces into the remaining oil to coat well, and mix in the white beans (drained and rinsed) and cherry tomatoes.

4. Place the chicken, beans and tomatoes on top of the aubergine and roast for 20 minutes or until the chicken is cooked through.

5. Serve to one bad-tempered American.

I will arise and go now,
and go to Innisfree,
And a small cabin build there,
of clay and wattles made:
Nine bean rows will I have there,
a hive for the honey bee,
And live alone in the
bee loud glade.

From 'The Lake Isle of Innisfree',
William Butler Yeats

BROAD BEAN AND CORNED BEEF HASH

I searched for a while to find out what Yeats might have made for dinner on his lonely lake isle from his nine rows of beans. It seems broad beans grow well in Ireland, and maybe if someone visited they could have brought him a few potatoes, a little butter and a can of corned beef as a special treat.

Serves 2–4

Ingredients

....

200 g can corned beef
75 g butter
4 potatoes
1 parsnip
500 g fresh broad beans
240 ml beef stock

Preparation

....

1. Heat the oven to 190°C while dicing the potatoes and parsnip.

2. Melt the butter in an ovenproof pan, and fry the potatoes and parsnip until browning and half-cooked.

3. Dice the corned beef and add to the pan with the beans.

4. Pour the stock over and place in the oven for 20 minutes or until it's all cooked through, stirring if necessary.

5. Season with salt and pepper.

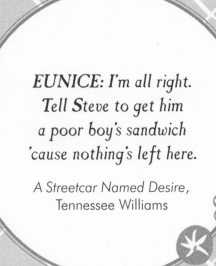

EUNICE: I'm all right.
Tell Steve to get him
a poor boy's sandwich
'cause nothing's left here.

A Streetcar Named Desire,
Tennessee Williams

NEW ORLEANS POOR BOY'S SANDWICH WITH SEAFOOD

Playwright Tennessee Williams, who won his first Pulitzer Prize for A Streetcar Named Desire, was born in Columbus, Mississippi, and moved to New Orleans at the age of 28. The city's life inspired the play about a poor family living in a tenement. You can use any kind of cooking oil for this, though peanut oil works particularly well, and you can use crawfish tails instead of shrimp or prawns.

Serves 3–4

Ingredients

1 wide, crusty baguette, cut into approximately 15-cm lengths, and split for sandwiches
Cooking oil (ideally peanut oil)
1 kg large peeled and cleaned prawns
Cajun seasoning – 1 tsp each paprika, cayenne, garlic salt, oregano, thyme, salt and pepper, blended
120 g plain flour
100 g cornmeal or fine breadcrumbs
1 egg, beaten
240 ml mayonnaise
Juice of ½ a lemon
Hot sauce to taste
Lettuce leaves and tomato slices

Preparation

....

1. Mix half of the seasoning with the flour and breadcrumbs, keeping half aside.

2. Dip each shrimp into the seasoning, then the beaten egg and then the flour mix, to coat.

3. Pour 1–2 cm oil into a deep frying pan. When the oil is medium–hot, fry the prawns until just browning and cooked through, about 4 minutes depending on the size of the prawn.

4. While the prawns are cooking, mix the lemon juice into the mayonnaise with a dash or two of hot sauce depending on your taste.

5. When the prawns are cooked, remove from the pan and drain on paper towels.

6. Spread the mayonnaise on the insides of the halved baguettes, and add salad garnish, then fill with the hot prawns and serve with extra hot sauce available on the side.

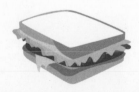

The Famed Sandwich of New Orleans

The most widely accepted story about the humble origins of New Orleans' po'boy sandwich attributes its invention to Clovis and Benjamin Martin, who had arrived from Louisiana, worked as streetcar conductors for several years and then opened their St Claude Avenue restaurant in the 1920s. The story goes that the brothers, in order to support the streetcar drivers who went on strike in 1929, started giving away the sandwiches – French bread filled with spare pieces of roast beef and gravy – free of charge out of the back of the restaurant to the striking workers, 'Members of Division 194'. The restaurant was open 24 hours a day and they went through around 1,000 loaves of bread each day.

Thus began the city's famous culinary tradition, which was clearly well known when Blanche DuBois took the streetcar named Desire in Tennessee Williams' 1947 play. The po'boy enjoyed a revival in popularity during the rebuilding from Hurricane Katrina and can be found all over the French Quarter in different guises as diverse as the city itself. The most popular today are fried seafood po'boys, made with shrimp, oyster, catfish and soft-shell crabs from the local gulf and bayous, while the poorest – or cheapest – are filled with French fries and gravy.

Nothing like mashed potatoes when you're feeling blue.

Heartburn, Nora Ephron

COMFORTING MASHED POTATOES

It's hardly surprising that the woman who wrote the screenplays for When Harry Met Sally, Sleepless in Seattle *and* Julie and Julia *knows just what you need when you're feeling weepy. In* Heartburn, *an autobiographical novel, her well-known love of food is at the forefront as the main character Rachel writes cookbooks for a living. She's also going through a bad marriage to a philanderer. She suggests adding a slice of butter to every forkful, but that's only if things look really bad.*

Serves 1

Ingredients

....

250 g potatoes, halved or quartered
2 tbsp butter
80 ml milk

Preparation

....

1. Boil the potatoes in water with a little salt (or just cry into the water) until tender and fragile (just like you).

2. Drain well, then mash, taking out all your feelings on those poor little potatoes.

3. Add the milk and most of the butter, and fluff the potatoes with a wooden spoon, adding salt and pepper to taste and a little more butter on the top, then place in your favourite bowl and tuck in.

4. The world will feel so much better for a while.

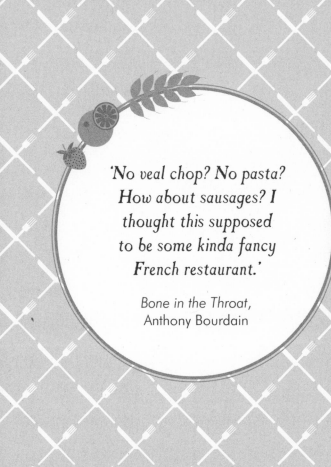

'No veal chop? No pasta?
How about sausages? I
thought this supposed
to be some kinda fancy
French restaurant.'

Bone in the Throat,
Anthony Bourdain

ITALIAN SAUSAGE PASTA
TO KEEP THE MAFIA HAPPY

Bone in the Throat *is a comic murder mystery set in a restaurant in Manhattan's Little Italy. Tommy is only the sous-chef and has to explain to mafioso Sally that they're a Mediterranean seafood restaurant, so they don't have any Italian food. What a pity. Sally would have been happy with some nice Italian sausage and pasta.*

Serves 2

Ingredients

Olive oil
1 medium onion
2 garlic cloves
300 g thick Italian beef sausages
Splash of dry wine, red or white
400 g chopped ripe tomatoes (use a tin if good fresh ones aren't available)
1 tbsp sun-dried tomatoes, chopped
200 g farfalle (bow-tie pasta) or pasta shells
Parmesan
Small bunch fresh basil

Preparation

1. Slit the sausages and squeeze the meat from the sausage casings, and discard the casings.

2. Heat a good glug of olive oil in a frying pan and add the onion, chopped, cooking until it starts to turn translucent.

3. Chop the garlic into small pieces and add to the pan, cooking for a couple of minutes before adding the sausage meat and stirring to let it brown.

4. After 10 minutes or so, add the wine and let it bubble, then all the tomatoes, then turn down to a simmer and cook for 15 minutes on a low heat.

5. Boil the pasta in salted water until tender, drain in a colander, then mix in the pan with the sauce.

6. Serve in bowls with torn basil leaves and grated Parmesan.

The Culinary Underbelly

Anthony Bourdain's bestselling memoir *Kitchen Confidential: Adventures in the Culinary Underbelly* is one of the most memorable books about food. The first of many books that would lift the lid on the life of a chef, it is gritty, dark and outspoken. In the kitchen of a good restaurant, you know your place and earn your scars. His pure, white-hot passion for food and its creation comes out on every page. Too lazy to peel fresh garlic, and thinking of buying it in a jar? 'You don't deserve to eat garlic.'

Bourdain was born in New York but his paternal grandparents were French, and his love of food began when he first tasted an oyster on a French fisherman's boat. He trained as a chef and worked in many Manhattan restaurants before his literary and television career began. *Bone in the Throat* was his first work of fiction and is set in a New York restaurant; it is peppered with culinary references, naturally: in Chapter One, the chefs are arguing about how to make a beurre blanc.

He sautéed lamb chops in red wine sauce and set the table outdoors in the afternoon.

The Girl with the Dragon Tattoo,
Stieg Larsson

LAMB CHOPS

*Mikael Blomkvist hardly ever bothers cooking for himself,
preferring to eat open sandwiches and drink copious amounts
of coffee while he works, so there's something very special
about this understated meal he cooks for Salander, showing
he cares. For a Scandinavian touch, add a tablespoon of
lingonberry jam to the sauce along with the wine and stock.*

Serves 2

Ingredients

Olive oil
4–6 lamb chops
2 cloves garlic, minced
3 tbsp fresh rosemary leaves
Salt and pepper

50 g shallots, chopped
125 ml full-bodied red wine
120 ml beef stock
2 tbsp butter
2 handfuls green beans

Preparation

1. Mix 1 tbsp olive oil in a bowl with the garlic and 1 tsp
    rosemary leaves.

2. Rub the lamb chops first with a little salt and pepper, then
    with the marinade, then set aside for 30 minutes.

3. Add a splash of olive oil to a small frying pan, just enough to coat the surface, then fry the shallots over a medium heat.

4. Add the wine and stock and simmer to reduce by half.

5. Add the butter and 2 tsp rosemary leaves.

6. In a separate hot frying pan, sear and sauté the lamb chops until browned on the outside and still a little pink inside.

7. Plate up and pour the sauce over the chops, serving with steamed green beans.

Some such regale now also in his thought,
With hasty steps his garden-ground he sought;
There delving with his hands, he first displaced
Four plants of garlick, large, and rooted fast;
The tender tops of parsley next he culls,
Then the old rue-bush shudders as he pulls,
And coriander last to these succeeds,
That hands on slightest threads her trembling seeds.
Placed near his sprightly fire, he now demands
The mortar at his sable servant's hands;
When stripping all his garlick first, he tore
The exterior coats, and cast them on the floor,
Then cast away with like contempt the skin,
Flimsier concealment of the cloves within.

From 'The Salad, by Virgil', William Cowper

PESTO TO PROVIDE AGAINST THE PANGS OF HUNGER

Attributed to the Roman poet Virgil, this poetic but homely description of the poor tenant farmer Simulus, hurrying to his kitchen garden to pull up herbs and grinding them up to make a green and white pesto sauce, has delighted epicureans for centuries. He adds to his herbs some salt, hard salty cheese, olive oil and vinegar; my favourite part of the long poem is where he uses his fingers to sweep up a 'small remnant from the mortar's side'. He eats his with bread, although of course you can use pasta. We are used to a basil and pine nut pesto these days, but ingredients for pesto are flexible so this is a version closer to Virgil's.

Serves 2

Ingredients

....

2 generous handfuls fresh basil leaves; alternatively, mix basil
   with spinach leaves, parsley, celery leaves, fresh coriander,
   thyme, oregano – any green herb found in your frugal
   garden
3 garlic cloves, chopped
1 tsp rock salt
150 g cheese such as pecorino or Romano, broken into pieces
120 ml extra virgin olive oil
1 tsp white wine vinegar

Preparation

....

1. Grind all the herbs, garlic and salt together using a large pestle and mortar (if you have a food processor, you may prefer to use it — Simulus probably would if he'd had one).

2. Add in the cheese and continue to mash together.

3. Gradually add in the olive oil and vinegar while mashing.

4. Serve stirred into pasta. If serving with bread for authenticity, use slightly less olive oil to make a thicker paste.

DESSERTS
AND SWEETS

To return to *Starters and Snacks*, go to p.7

This troop he had led out on gypsy excursions to Halsell Wood at nutting-time, and since the cold weather had set in he had taken them on a clear day to gather sticks for a bonfire in the hollow of a hillside, where he drew out a small feast of gingerbread for them, and improvised a Punch-and-Judy drama with some private home-made puppets.

Middlemarch, George Eliot

GINGERBREAD CAKE FOR A COLD WEATHER FEAST

The idea of treacle gingerbread cake reminds me of Hallowe'en parties, when pieces of gingerbread were dipped in treacle and hung from strings for us to eat with our hands behind our backs – messy and delicious. The following recipe for gingerbread is adapted from a cookbook published in the 1850s.

Serves 12

Ingredients

180 g light brown sugar
240 g butter
240 g treacle or molasses
240 g golden syrup
240 ml warm milk
6 eggs, beaten
720 g plain flour

2 tsp bicarbonate of soda
2 tbsp ground ginger
1 tsp grated nutmeg
1 tsp grated orange zest
½ tsp salt
240 ml hot water

Preparation

1. Preheat the oven to 180°C and butter a large baking tin.

2. In a bowl, cream the sugar together with the butter, and mix in the treacle, syrup and milk.

3. In another bowl, sift together the flour with the bicarbonate of soda, ginger and nutmeg, orange zest and salt.

4. Add a little at a time of the eggs and a little of the flour mixture to the butter and sugar mixture, combining all gradually.

5. Stir in the hot water, and pour the mixture into the tin.

6. Bake for 45 minutes to 1 hour until a skewer comes out clean, then allow to cool before serving.

Poetic Puddings

The American poet Emily Dickinson (1830–1886) enjoyed baking for her family in Amherst, Massachusetts. Her friend Thomas Wentworth Higginson quoted her as saying, 'People must have puddings.' She wrote a poem on the back of a recipe for coconut cake, and drafted another poem on the back of a baking-chocolate wrapper. In one letter she mentioned she was 'pleased the gingerbread triumphed'.

Her poem '"Hope" is the Thing with Feathers' ends:

> *Yet, never, in Extremity,*
> *It asked a crumb – of Me.*

Farther on he beheld great fields of Indian corn, with its golden ears peeping from hasty pudding; and the yellow pumpkins lying beneath them, turning up their fair round bellies to the sun, and giving ample prospects of the most luxurious of pies; and anon he passed the fragrant buckwheat fields, breathing the odour of the beehive, and as he beheld them, soft anticipations stole over his mind of dainty slapjacks, well buttered and garnished with honey or treacle, by the delicate little dimpled hand of Katrina Van Tassel.

The Legend of Sleepy Hollow, Washington Irving

DAINTY BUCKWHEAT SLAPJACKS GARNISHED BY A DELICATE HAND

A slapjack is like a buckwheat pancake, fried on a griddle and served with butter and honey; a classic American prairie breakfast, but also a delicious sweet treat at any time.

Serves 4

Ingredients

2 tbsp butter
240 g buckwheat flour
60 g plain flour
2 tbsp brown sugar
1 tbsp baking powder
1 tsp sea salt

240 ml milk
2 large eggs
Olive oil

To serve:
Butter
Honey

Preparation

1. Melt and then cool the butter and set aside.

2. Mix all the dry ingredients in a large bowl and form a well in the centre.

3. Beat the eggs, butter and milk, pour into the well of the flour mix and stir lightly to form a batter.

4. Heat a lightly oiled griddle or frying pan and drop about a quarter of the batter onto the griddle per pancake.

5. Cook for 2–3 minutes, until bubbles appear on top and the edges are set, then flip and cook until browning and cooked through.

6. Serve with butter and honey.

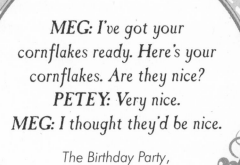

MEG: *I've got your cornflakes ready. Here's your cornflakes. Are they nice?*
PETEY: *Very nice.*
MEG: *I thought they'd be nice.*

The Birthday Party,
Harold Pinter

VERY NICE BIRTHDAY PARTY CORNFLAKE CLUSTERS

This excerpt is classic Pinter, from one of his best-known plays. You can just feel the awkwardness and absurdity of the scene in a run-down seaside boarding house as Meg tries to please her husband by offering him... a nice bowl of cornflakes. Personally, I think they'd be a whole lot nicer covered in butter, syrup and chocolate – especially for Stanley's birthday party.

Makes 16

Ingredients

100 g butter
140 ml golden syrup
2 tbsp cocoa powder (not drinking chocolate)
120 g cornflakes

Preparation

1. Melt the butter in a saucepan over a low heat.

2. Add golden syrup, and continue to heat and stir until bubbling.

3. Sprinkle the cocoa powder in and continue to mix well over the heat, until smooth and syrupy with enough chocolate flavour.

4. Pour the cornflakes in little by little, stirring gently, until the liquid is coating the cornflakes and there's none to spare.

5. Spoon into paper cases and leave to set for an awkward Pinterian pause of an hour or two.

Season of mists and mellow fruitfulness,
Close bosom-friend of the maturing sun;
Conspiring with him how to load and bless
With fruit the vines that round the thatch-eaves run;
To bend with apples the moss'd cottage-trees,
And fill all fruit with ripeness to the core;
To swell the gourd, and plump the hazel shells
With a sweet kernel.

From 'To Autumn', John Keats

MELLOW FRUITFULNESS
HAZELNUT CRISP

*This simple dessert combines fruit with hazelnuts:
I'm sure Keats would have approved.*

Serves 4–6

Ingredients

....

8 pears
180 g brown sugar
60 g hazelnuts
120 g plain flour

45 g rolled oats
Pinch salt
120 g butter

Preparation

....

1. Preheat oven to 180°C.

2. Peel the pears and cut the flesh away from the cores and stalks, discarding them, then roughly chop the flesh.

3. Sprinkle with 90 g sugar in a baking dish, and set aside.

4. Break the hazelnuts into small pieces using a food processor, pestle and mortar, or putting them in a plastic bag and using a rolling pin. Mix them with the other 90 g of sugar, and flour, oats and salt.

5. Break the butter into small pieces and mix with the dry ingredients into a crumble topping.

6. Spread the topping over the pears, and bake for 30 minutes until browning nicely on top.

And when I brought out the baked apples from the closet, and hoped our friends would be so very obliging as to take some, 'Oh!' said he, directly, 'there is nothing in the way of fruit half so good, and these are the finest looking home-baked apples I ever saw in my life.' That, you know, was so very... And I am sure, by his manner, it was no compliment. Indeed they are very delightful apples, and Mrs Wallis does them full justice – only we do not have them baked more than twice, and Mr Woodhouse made us promise to have them done three times – but Miss Woodhouse will be so good as not to mention it.

Emma, Jane Austen

BAKED APPLES

Baked apples are delicious and very easy to make. This combines a recipe from Jane Austen's day with a few simple ingredients you may have in your kitchen.

Serves 4

Ingredients

125 ml glass red wine
12 cloves
4 large cooking apples or firm, tart apples such as
  Granny Smith
Juice and zest of 1 lemon
Handful sultanas
Handful toasted almonds or pecans
1 tbsp brown sugar
1 tbsp cinnamon

To serve:
Whipping cream, double cream or vanilla ice cream

Preparation

1. Preheat the oven to 180°C.

2. Place the cloves in the glass of wine.

3. Use an apple-corer or sharp knife to remove the cores from the apples and place them whole into a baking dish into which they fit snugly. Drizzle lemon juice into their centres, then mix any remaining juice with the zest, sultanas, almonds or pecans, sugar and cinnamon and stuff the apple centres with the mixture.

4. Pour the wine and cloves over the top and cover with baking foil.

5. Place in the oven for 15 minutes, then remove the foil and bake for another approximately 15 minutes. The timing will depend on the size of the apples: they should be soft but not mushy.

6. Serve in bowls with a dollop of the cream of choice.

Morning and evening
Maids heard the goblins cry:
'Come buy our orchard fruits,
Come buy, come buy:
Apples and quinces,
Lemons and oranges,
Plump unpeck'd cherries,
Melons and raspberries,
Bloom-down-cheek'd peaches,
Swart-headed mulberries,
Wild free-born cranberries,
Crab-apples, dewberries,
Pineapples, blackberries,
Apricots, strawberries;
All ripe together
In summer weather.'

From 'Goblin Market', Christina Rossetti

SWEET TEMPTATION:
QUINCE PRESERVED IN HONEY

Sisters Lizzie and Laura hear the calls of the goblins selling their tempting fruits when they go to fetch water. But Lizzie warns Laura of the perils of giving in, telling of a friend who pined away to her death after buying goblin fruit, since she was unable to get more. Quinces and apples are often associated with temptation (see p.175) and this recipe for preserving quince in honey – as mentioned in literature since ancient times – will allow you to indulge yourself whenever you like.

Serves enough to keep the goblins away

Ingredients

2.3 kg quince
1.4 kg honey
720 ml water
5–6 grinds of black pepper

Preparation

1. Peel and quarter the quinces, remove the cores and slice thinly. You should be left with around 1.4 kg fruit.

2. Combine the honey and water in a large pan over a low heat to form a syrup.

3.   Add the quince, return to the boil and then reduce to a simmer, skimming off any foam.

4.   Turn the fruit gently from time to time without breaking it. The fruit should turn soft and pink after about 30 minutes.

5.   Grind in the black pepper and continue cooking for about another 15 minutes until the fruit is turning translucent, pink and pliable.

6.   If you want the preserve to keep for months, spoon it into jars, ensuring there are no air pockets, and top up with syrup but leave a 1 cm air gap at the top.

7.   Seal the jars and process in a hot water bath (you can find instructions online).

8.   Eat with cream or vanilla ice cream, or add to a fruit dessert.

Forbidden Fruits

The quince has been cultivated from ancient times, originating in Persia and Anatolia. The ancient Greeks obtained a common variety from Cydon in Crete, so the fruit was known as *Cydonia*, from which the English word quince derives. In the first century AD, Pliny wrote of the fruit being preserved in honey.

Because it was a golden-yellow colour and widely cultivated in the East and around Palestine, many scholars believe that references to a fruit in the scriptures and early literature, commonly translated as 'apple', was in fact a quince: the forbidden fruit of the Garden of Eden, for example, and the golden apple that Paris presented to Aphrodite. The quince had strong connections with fertility, love and marriage – in *Plutarch's Lives*, Solon decreed that 'bride and bridegroom shall be shut into a chamber, and eat a quince together' – and continued to have such associations in medieval England.

Quince cheese, or *dulce de membrillo*, is a sweet jelly eaten in Spain and Portugal. In Portuguese, the quince is called *marmelo* and the jelly *marmelada*, from which we get the word marmalade; orange marmalade didn't arrive until 1790 when it was invented in Scotland.

In *The Book of Salt* by Vietnamese-American author Monique Truong (2003), 'quinces remain a fruit, hard and obstinate… until they are simmered, coddled for hours above a low, steady flame.' Its dry flesh soaks up the honey and water, becoming an opulent orange.

As he ate his breakfast, Monseigneur Welcome remarked gaily to his sister, who said nothing, and to Madame Magloire, who was grumbling under her breath, that one really does not need either fork or spoon, even of wood, in order to dip a bit of bread in a cup of milk.

Les Misérables, Victor Hugo

BREAD AND BUTTER PUDDING TO FEED THE HUNGRY

The novel by Victor Hugo is full of references to bread as a staple necessity for life. When your bread starts to go stale, douse it in milk and make bread and butter pudding.

Serves 6

Ingredients

....

5 eggs
1 litre whole milk
100 g sugar
1 tsp vanilla extract
¼ tsp ground cinnamon
¼ tsp grated nutmeg
8 thick slices day-old bread
40 g butter
100 g sultanas

Preparation

....

1. Preheat the oven to 180°C and grease a medium-sized baking dish (approximately 17x28 cm, 5 cm deep).

2. In a bowl, whisk together the eggs, milk, half the sugar, vanilla extract, cinnamon and nutmeg.

3. Cut the bread into triangles and butter each side, then arrange in the dish, ensuring the base of the dish is fully covered, and scatter the sultanas as you go to ensure they are spread evenly.

4. Pour the egg mixture over the bread, sprinkle the rest of the sugar on top, and bake for 40 minutes or so until golden.

She got up, unlocked a drawer, and taking from it a parcel wrapped in paper, disclosed presently to our eyes a good-sized seed cake.

'I meant to give each of you some of this to take with you,' said she, 'but as there is so little toast, you must have it now,' and she proceeded to cut slices with a generous hand.

We feasted that evening as on nectar and ambrosia; and not the least delight of the entertainment was the smile of gratification with which our hostess regarded us, as we satisfied our famished appetites on the delicate fare she liberally supplied.

Jane Eyre, Charlotte Brontë

AMBROSIAL CARAWAY SEED CAKE FOR FAMISHED APPETITES

Jane has been sent to Lowood School for Girls, after the loss first of her parents and then, as if that weren't enough (as Oscar Wilde's Lady Bracknell might say, 'to lose both looks like carelessness'), the death of her guardian and uncle. Humiliated by the headmaster, she finds kindness finally when her teacher, Miss Temple, invites Jane and her friend Helen for tea in her parlour. Caraway seed, also known as meridian fennel or Persian cumin, is used in a wide variety of cuisines. Serve to your guests liberally, with a smile.

Ingredients

120 g warmed butter
120 g caster sugar
3 large eggs
175 g self-raising flour

2 rounded tsp caraway seeds
50 g ground almonds
3 tbsp milk

Preparation

1. Preheat the oven to 180°C and line a tin with greaseproof paper.

2. Cream the butter with the sugar until fluffy.

3. Beat the eggs into the butter and sugar, then sieve the flour into it, add the seeds, almonds and milk, and mix together to a creamy consistency.

4. Spoon into the tin and level the surface.

5. Bake in the middle of the oven for 1 hour until it feels firm and a skewer comes out dry.

6. Allow to rest for 10 minutes, then turn it out onto a wire rack.

Seed Cakes

Caraway seed cake, with its aniseed flavour, was a Victorian favourite and continued to crop up in literature well into the twentieth century, for example in J. R. R. Tolkien's *The Hobbit*, where Bilbo Baggins feeds his guests with 'two beautiful round seed cakes which he had baked that afternoon'. It featured delightfully in *David Copperfield* by Charles Dickens: 'I cut and handed the sweet seed cake – the little sisters had a bird-like fondness for picking up seeds and pecking at sugar.'

The first recorded mention of seed cake in English was in 1570 in *A Hundreth Good Pointes of Husbandrie* by Thomas Tusser:

'Wife, some time this weeke if that all thing go cleare,
an ende of wheat sowing we make for this yeare.
Remember you therefore, though I do it not,
the Seede Cake, the Pasties, and Furmentie pot.'

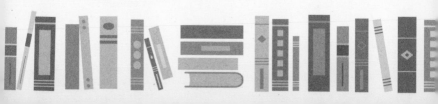

She prepared a meal of
cheese and barley
and amber honey mixed
with **P**ramnian wine.

The Odyssey, Homer

EPIC CHEESE
AND HONEY PIES

*The combined flavours of the cheese and honey in these
traditional pies from Sfakia in Crete hark back to ancient
Greece. They can be eaten as a dessert or a snack, and go well
with a strong wine or liqueur such as raki. Mizithra is a soft,
dry, crumbly white cheese; if it's unavailable, you can find feta
with the same texture, though the flavour will be different.*

Makes 15 pies

Ingredients

1 egg
240 ml water
120 ml olive oil
1 tsp salt
1 kg plain flour

1 kg mizithra cheese
Cooking oil
Clear, amber-coloured
    pouring honey

Preparation

1. Mix the egg, water, olive oil and salt together in a bowl,
   then add the flour and knead to form a soft pastry dough,
   elastic but not sticky. Set it aside for 30 minutes to allow
   it to become more elastic.

2. Take a knob of dough the size of a small apple and press it out into the size of a saucer.

3. Put a golf ball-sized piece of mizithra into the middle, pull the sides of the dough around it and hide the cheese inside the pastry ball.

4. Lightly roll the pastry out into a flat circle as thin as you can – less than 1 cm – with the cheese spread out evenly inside and not spilling out (if this isn't working for your pastry, then you can simply roll out two thin circles of pastry, put the cheese inside, and seal the edges).

5. Stack the pies, separated by greaseproof paper, until all the pastry is used up.

6. Heat the cooking oil in a frying pan and cook one pie at a time until it starts to brown and bubble, then flip to do the other side.

7. When done, serve with honey poured over.

Epic Temptations

Food and wine often serve as temptations to Odysseus, in the poem by Homer, as he attempts to travel home to Ithaka, and his wife and palace, after ten long years of war at Troy. The best known symbol of food as temptation in the epic poem is the lotus fruit, which causes Odysseus' men to forget their journey and homeland. When they come to the cave of the Cyclops and some of the men try to steal some milk and whey, again giving in to their appetites, the monster dashes out their brains; while the Cyclops himself is intoxicated with wine, Odysseus manages to effect his escape. Meanwhile, the suitors who want to take over Odysseus' estate and wife back home are lazily gorging themselves on feasts.

While Odysseus (like James Bond) could easily resist the food and drink that were the downfall of other men, he was helpless when a beautiful woman was on the menu. Circe, the seductress and sorceress, treats his men like kings but adds 'her own vile pinch' to the honey mixed with wine to make them forget their home, then transforms them into pigs. Odysseus escapes this spell, yet still stays with Circe for almost a year. When at last he leaves, she still implores him to remain with her and share her food and wine.

Centuries later, in the epic poem *The Aeneid* by the Roman Virgil (70–19 BC), Aeneas also throws a cake dripping with oozing honey but laced with 'poppies drowsy with slumber' to the monster Cerberus to drug him so that he can pass. It's easy to imagine being tricked by a poppy seed cake dripping with honey.

HELMER: Not been
nibbling sweets?
NORA: No, certainly not.
HELMER: Not even taken a
bite at a macaroon or two?

A Doll's House, Henrik Ibsen

FRENCH MACAROONS FOR SURREPTITIOUS NIBBLING

Ibsen provides us with a perfect excuse to make French macaroons, little round meringue sandwiches with buttercream filling.

Ingredients

300 g icing sugar
300 g ground almonds
Pinch salt
5 egg whites
55 g caster sugar
Food colouring

For the buttercream filling:
250 g unsalted butter
150 g icing sugar

Preparation

1. Sieve the ground almonds, icing sugar and salt into a bowl, discarding any large pieces of almond.

2. In another bowl, beat the egg whites and caster sugar until stiff.

3. Add food colouring and continue to beat briefly until blended, then fold dry ingredients into the egg whites to make a smooth mix.

4. Pipe into 1.5-cm rounds on trays lined with non-stick baking paper.

5. Set them aside for 1 hour, then heat the oven to 150°C and bake for 20 minutes until they come off the paper easily.

6. Refrigerating them for 24 hours will make them chewier and tastier.

7. For the filling, beat the butter until pale and fluffy, then sift the icing sugar into the butter gradually, beating until mixed well. Spoon a little of the filling in between two rounds and sandwich them together.

Many years had elapsed during which nothing of Combray, save what was comprised in the theatre and the drama of my going to bed there, had any existence for me, when one day in winter, as I came home, my mother, seeing that I was cold, offered me some tea, a thing I did not ordinarily take. I declined at first, and then, for no particular reason, changed my mind. She sent out for one of those short, plump little cakes called 'petites madeleines', which look as though they had been moulded in the fluted scallop of a pilgrim's shell. And soon, mechanically, weary after a dull day with the prospect of a depressing morrow, I raised to my lips a spoonful of the tea in which I had soaked a morsel of the cake. No sooner had the warm liquid, and the crumbs with it, touched my palate than a shudder ran through my whole body, and I stopped, intent upon the extraordinary changes that were taking place. An exquisite pleasure had invaded my senses, but individual, detached, with no suggestion of its origin. And at once the vicissitudes of life had become indifferent to me, its disasters innocuous, its brevity illusory – this new sensation having had on me the effect which love has of filling me with a precious essence; or rather this essence was not in me, it was myself. I had ceased now to feel mediocre, accidental, mortal.

Remembrance of Things Past, Marcel Proust

MADELEINES TO REMEMBER

These quintessentially French cakes are certain to cheer you on a dreary day, and are perfect as an accompaniment to your coffee or afternoon tea.

Makes 24

Ingredients

....

100 g unsalted butter
2 eggs
Pinch salt
65 g sugar
½ tsp vanilla extract
1 tbsp lemon zest
60 g plain flour
Icing sugar to decorate

Preparation

....

1. Preheat oven to 170°C.

2. Use a little of the butter to grease a madeleine tray, ensuring you get all the crevices of the scallop shells.

3. Melt the rest of the butter in a saucepan, allowing it almost to turn toasty brown without burning, then remove from heat and allow to cool to room temperature.

4. Add the eggs and salt to a bowl and beat until doubled in volume.

5. Continue beating as you add the sugar, until it is dissolved, then add the vanilla extract and the lemon zest.

6. Sieve the flour into the bowl and mix it into the batter slowly.

7. Stir the cooled butter into the mix, then rest the batter for 1 hour.

8. Fill each scallop shell two-thirds full with the batter, and bake for 10–12 minutes or until starting to brown at the edges.

9. Remove from the baking trays and allow to cool on a wire rack, before dusting with icing sugar.

Tess wished to abridge her visit as much as possible; but the young man was pressing, and she consented to accompany him. He conducted her about the lawns, and flower beds, and conservatories; and thence to the fruit garden and greenhouses, where he asked her if she liked strawberries.

'Yes,' said Tess, 'when they come.'

'They are already here.' D'Urberville began gathering specimens of the fruit for her, handing them back to her as he stooped; and, presently, selecting a specially fine product of the 'British Queen' variety, he stood up and held it by the stem to her mouth.

Tess of the D'Urbervilles, Thomas Hardy

A (STRAWBERRY) FOOL FOR LOVE

What is it about summer fruit and metaphors of desire? It's almost too much when this suave, wealthy chap insists on placing the strawberry in poor, shy Tess' mouth leaving her 'in a slight distress', foreshadowing the way he will seduce her. No wonder Hardy was considered scandalous in his day.

Serves 2

Ingredients

120 ml whipping cream, chilled
1 tbsp sugar
½ tsp vanilla extract

7 strawberries, hulled, plus two nicely-shaped ones for garnish

Preparation

1. Place the strawberries in a bowl, sprinkle with sugar and vanilla extract, mash the fruit lightly and leave to stand for a few minutes.

2. Pour the cream into a bowl and beat until light and fluffy.

3. Fold half the strawberry mix into the cream.

4. Layer the fool and the strawberry mix in the bowls.

5. Top with the reserved strawberries, so you can hold them up to one another's lips.

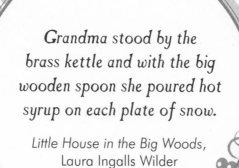

Grandma stood by the brass kettle and with the big wooden spoon she poured hot syrup on each plate of snow.

Little House in the Big Woods,
Laura Ingalls Wilder

BECAUSE MAPLE SYRUP NEVER HURT ANYBODY

This novel for children is the first in the 'Little House on the Prairie' series, and is based on the author's childhood memories of rural life in the northern United States in the 1870s, describing the old homesteading skills such as making confections from the maple syrup harvested from the trees around them. This delightful scene is one that many readers remember and go back to.

Ingredients

Maple syrup
Snow (but if you don't have any snow to hand, see below)

Preparation

1. First, wait for snow. Heat the maple syrup in a pan. When the stars are clear in the sky, and your breath is like smoke in the frosty air, scoop up clean snow with your plate. Pour hot maple syrup onto the snow and let it cool into candy.

2. You can also make maple candy without the snow: in a heavy saucepan, bring the maple syrup to boil gradually, stirring, until it reaches 110°C (testing it with a thermometer).

3. Remove from the heat and cool for about 10 minutes, without stirring, to 80°C.

4. Stir rapidly with the wooden spoon for 5 minutes until it becomes light, creamy and fudge-like, and pour into moulds.

5. Set aside to cool.

Angel cake, that melted in the mouth, and his rather stodgier companion bursting with peel and raisins.

Rebecca, Daphne du Maurier

MELT-IN-THE-MOUTH ANGEL FOOD CAKE

While British angel cake tends to be three colours and made with icing and filling, The Complete Illustrated Cookery Book *published in 1934 lists an 'angel cake' recipe with no colouring and the list of ingredients of today's American version. So it seems likely that the teas at Manderley had something closer to the American angel food cake. The cream of tartar helps the beaten egg whites to retain their stiffness even at high temperatures. You will need an angel food cake pan, non-greased, as grease prevents the cake from rising.*

Serves 8

Ingredients

210 g plain flour
300 g caster sugar
12 eggs, separated (egg whites only)

1½ tsp cream of tartar
½ tsp salt
Zest of 1½ lemons
¾ tsp vanilla essence

Preparation

1. Preheat oven to 180°C.

2. Sift together several times the flour and 75 g sugar and set aside.

3. Put the egg whites (they should be room temperature) in a bowl with the cream of tartar and salt and whip until they start to foam and thicken (about 2 minutes if using an electric whisk). Add lemon zest, vanilla and remaining 225 g sugar, and continue to whip the mix until forming stiff, glossy peaks.

4. Fold the flour mixture into it carefully.

5. Scoop the batter into the tin, cut through the batter twice with a knife or spatula to eliminate any large air pockets, smooth the top, and bake for 40–50 minutes. A skewer should come out clean.

6. Remove from the oven and turn it upside down, still in the tin, to cool.

7. Set upright and use a knife to loosen the cake from the tin. Serve at teatime with whipped cream and raspberries or any fresh soft fruit.

8. Dream of going to Manderley again.

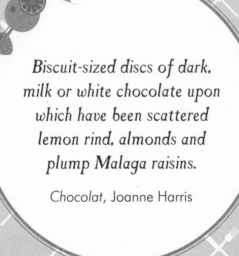

Biscuit-sized discs of dark, milk or white chocolate upon which have been scattered lemon rind, almonds and plump Malaga raisins.

Chocolat, Joanne Harris

CHOCOLATE MENDIANTS

Why are these delightful French confections called mendicants or beggars? Because the nuts and fruits (raisins, hazelnuts, figs and almonds) with which they were traditionally decorated were chosen to represent the colours of monastic robes, and the monks lived from the charity of others.

Ingredients

Good quality chocolate (for a party, use a variety of white, milk and dark)
Preserved lemon peel, cut into small pieces
Almonds, broken into pieces
Raisins

Preparation

1. Line a baking tray with baking paper.

2. Melt the chocolate until smooth in a bain-marie (a bowl or pan placed over a saucepan of simmering water). If using different chocolates, you will need to melt them in separate bowls.

3. Drop a teaspoonful of chocolate onto parchment paper so that it forms a biscuit-sized disc. Do six at a time, allowing them to set a little before lightly pressing the fruit and nuts into them. You may need to reheat the chocolate to keep it liquid.

4. Allow the chocolate to set for 15–30 minutes before serving.

Each piece was sweet and light to the very centre and Edmund had never tasted anything more delicious.

The Lion, the Witch and the Wardrobe, C. S. Lewis

MAGICAL TURKISH DELIGHT

An enchanted and addictive version of Turkish delight is given to Edmund by the evil White Queen, which enables her to learn information about his family. For it to be light to the very centre it should be eaten fresh.

Makes 18 pieces

Ingredients

....

300 g caster sugar
1 tsp cream of tartar
1 tbsp powdered gelatine
2 tbsp rosewater
¼ tsp pink food colouring
100 g icing sugar
120 g cornflour

Preparation

....

1. Put 125 ml water into a saucepan, add the sugar and cream of tartar, and stir over a medium heat to dissolve the sugar.

2. Bring to the boil and cook for 15 minutes or until it reaches 125°C on a sugar thermometer, then remove from the heat.

3. In a bowl, whisk gelatine powder into 80 ml boiling water to dissolve, then add another 80 ml water, rosewater and food colouring.

4. Strain this liquid into the sugar syrup and mix together.

5. Pour into a greased loaf tin and refrigerate for 4 hours until set.

6. Sift the icing sugar with the cornflour.

7. Dust a chopping board with a little of the icing sugar mix. Turn the Turkish delight out and chop into 18 cubes using an oiled knife.

8. Toss with the rest of the icing sugar mix.

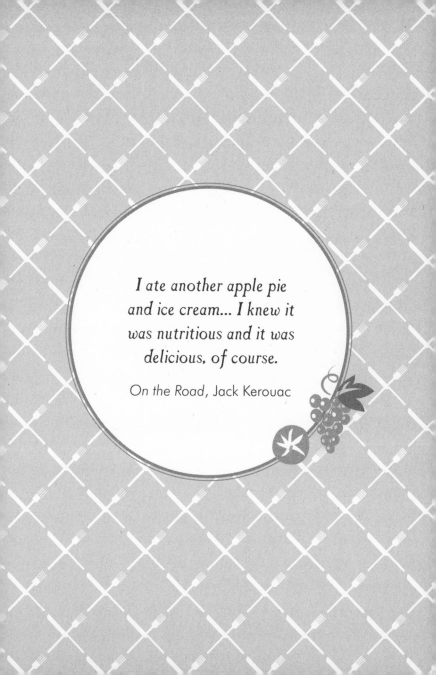

*I ate another apple pie
and ice cream... I knew it
was nutritious and it was
delicious, of course.*

On the Road, Jack Kerouac

APPLE PIE FOR PRETTY GIRLS AND APPRECIATIVE BOYS

When Sal first travels west across America from New York, catching buses and hitchhiking, he soon runs low on cash and the only affordable thing to eat on the road is apple pie and ice cream. As he gets deeper into Iowa, the pie gets better, 'the ice cream richer' and the girls prettier.

Serves 4

Ingredients

For the pie crust:
300 g plain flour (plus a little extra for rolling)
1 tsp salt
2 tsp sugar
300 g cold butter cut into 1-cm cubes
120 ml sour cream
A little milk or egg yolk

For the filling:
1.5 kg cooking apples (6–8 apples)
1 tsp lemon juice or cider vinegar
90 g brown sugar
3 tbsp plain flour
¼ tsp ground allspice
¼ tsp grated nutmeg
½ tsp ground cinnamon
1 tsp vanilla extract

Preparation

....

1. In a bowl, mix the flour, salt and sugar.

2. Add cubes of butter and work into the flour with your fingers until the butter pieces are very small.

3. Add the sour cream and mix together with a fork until it begins to form a dough.

4. Put it on a floured work surface, roll into a ball, then cut in half and leave in the fridge wrapped in cling film for 1 hour to rest.

5. For the filling, peel, core and slice the apples into a bowl, adding the lemon juice or vinegar to prevent them from browning.

6. In another bowl combine the flour, sugar and spices, then use your fingers to coat the apples with the mixture, adding the vanilla extract.

7. Preheat the oven to 200°C.

8. Remove one half of the pastry from the fridge, leave to rest for ten minutes and then roll it out on the floured surface to fit a 20-cm pie dish, leaving a little overhang around the edges when you press it down into the dish. Fill with the apples – they should be higher than the rim of the dish.

9. Roll out the second half of the pastry until it will cover the pie, again leaving an overhang, and crimp at the edges to seal. Cut slits in the top and brush with milk or beaten egg yolk.

10. Bake in the middle of the oven, putting a baking sheet underneath to catch any drips. After 15 minutes, reduce the heat to 180°C and bake for another 45 minutes or until the juice is bubbling up through the vents.

11. The pastry should be golden; if it's cooking too quickly on top, drape a sheet of foil over the top.

12. Allow to cool for 1 hour, and serve a la mode.

A Slice of the Pie

In literature, who ate all the pies? It seems everyone likes a slice of pie, century after century.

Back in 1590, the English dramatist and poet Robert Green wrote as a compliment to a lady, 'Thy breath is like the steame of apple-pyes.' The Irish writer Jonathan Swift popularised the expression, in 1738, 'Promises and pie-crust are made to be broken,' though any kind of pie would presumably do. And in 1815, Jane Austen wrote in a letter to Cassandra, 'Good apple pies are a considerable part of our domestic happiness.'

In John Steinbeck's *East of Eden*, published just a few years before *On the Road* in 1952, Tom is equally passionate about blueberry pie. '"No pies for three months." Tom said, "We can't get through it. We'll have to move to another place."'

Is there anything as sweet as cherry pie, or more American than apple pie? Actually, serving apple pie 'a la mode', with ice cream, is what makes it North American. Since eating apples didn't arrive in the New World until the seventeenth century and even then weren't used initially for pies, blueberry pie is arguably more American.

Some say that the best pie scene in twentieth-century literature is in Roald Dahl's *Danny, the Champion of the World*. Doctor Spencer calls when Danny is ravenous and leaves him 'the most enormous and beautiful pie in the world', with rich, golden pastry – a cold meat pie with hard-boiled eggs buried inside.

"They can add cream if they like later, I mean we've nothing really against it though it's not nutritionally necessary."

The Edible Woman, Margaret Atwood

DEFINITELY NATURAL
RICE PUDDING

Marian is working for a market research firm, who need another 'pre-test taster for the canned rice pudding study' and has to answer questions about whether the colour seems Natural, Somewhat Artificial or Definitely Unnatural. They make it sound clinically unappealing, so I offer as an alternative this fresh and healthy version.

Serves 4

Ingredients

480 ml water
190 g brown rice
Pinch salt
960 ml milk
2 tbsp sugar (alternatively honey or maple syrup)
1 pinch ground cardamom
1 tsp vanilla extract
2 tbsp unsalted butter
Optional:
100 g raisins

Preparation

....

1. First cook the rice, following the packet instructions.

2. Rinse the rice in cold water and set it aside.

3. Warm the milk, sugar, cardamom and vanilla in a pan over a low heat, stirring as you bring it to a boil.

4. Add the rice, butter and raisins, stir and simmer for about 30 minutes, ensuring it doesn't stick, until it reduces to a creamy consistency.

5. You can add cream to serve, although it's not nutritionally necessary.

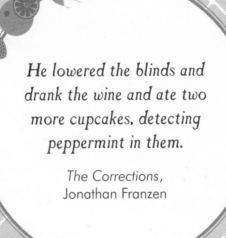

He lowered the blinds and drank the wine and ate two more cupcakes, detecting peppermint in them.

The Corrections,
Jonathan Franzen

PEPPERMINT MOCHA CUPCAKES TO CORRECT WHATEVER IS WRONG

When Melissa brings her college professor Chip a plate of cupcakes, he is suspicious and asks why. She doesn't answer – just leaves them on his doormat and says chirpily that he can do what he likes with them. Chip is not at his best at that moment. But he opens a bottle of Chardonnay and starts to eat them.

Makes 12–15

Ingredients

200 g sugar
90 g plus 2 tbsp plain flour
30 g plus 1 tbsp unsweetened cocoa
¾ tsp baking powder
¾ tsp baking soda
½ tsp fine salt
1 large egg, at room temperature
120 ml milk

60 ml vegetable oil
¼ tsp vanilla extract
120 ml hot black coffee

For the icing:
240 g unsalted butter, room temperature
250 g icing sugar
2 tbsp milk
1 tsp vanilla extract
¼ tsp peppermint extract

Preparation

....

1. Preheat the oven to 180°C and line the muffin tins with paper cases.

2. For the cake mix, whisk the sugar, flour, cocoa, baking powder and salt in a bowl.

3. In another bowl whisk the egg, milk, oil and vanilla.

4. Add the wet to the dry ingredients and whisk to a thick batter, but don't overbeat.

5. Add the coffee and stir to combine.

6. Three-quarters fill the cupcake liners with the batter and bake for 20 minutes or less until just firm on top. A skewer should come out clean and dry.

7. Let the cakes cool in the tin for 10 minutes, then remove and cool completely before icing.

8. For the icing, beat the butter until light and fluffy, add the sugar, milk, vanilla and peppermint, and continue to cream until the right consistency, adjusting if necessary with extra sugar or milk.

9. Pipe or spoon the icing onto the cakes, and serve with a glass of Chardonnay if you wish.

CONVERSION TABLES

All the conversions in the tables below are close approximates, which have been rounded up or down. When using a recipe always stick to one measurement; do not alternate between them.

OVEN TEMPERATURES

°C	°F	Mark
140	275	1
150	300	2
170	325	3
180	350	4
190	375	5
200	400	6
220	425	7
230	450	8
240	475	9

WEIGHTS

Imperial	Metric
½ oz	10 g
¾ oz	20 g
1 oz	25 g
1½ oz	40 g
2 oz	50 g
2½ oz	60 g
3 oz	75 g
4 oz	110 g
4½ oz	125 g
5 oz	150 g
6 oz	175 g
7 oz	200 g
8 oz	225 g
9 oz	250 g
10 oz	275 g
12 oz	350 g
1 lb	450 g
1 lb 8 oz	700 g
2 lb	900 g
3 lb	1.35 kg

INDEX

If you're interested in finding out more about our books,
find us on Facebook at **Summersdale Publishers**
and follow us on Twitter at **@Summersdale**.

www.summersdale.com